WISDOM FOR MARRIAGE
MADE SIMPLE

WISDOM FOR MARRIAGE
MADE SIMPLE

Praying Medic

INKITY
PRESS™

Inkity Press LLC

137 East Elliot Road, #2292, Gilbert, AZ 85299

This book and other Inkity Press titles can be found at: PrayingMedic.com

For more information visit our website at **www.inkitypress.com** or email us at **admin@inkitypress.com** or **admin@prayingmedic.com**

ISBN-13: 978-1-947968-25-7 (Inkity Press)

Printed in the U.S.A.

To Erika and Charlie

TABLE OF CONTENTS

WE NEVER SET OUT TO write a book about marriage. In fact, if you had told either of us twenty years ago that we'd be co-authoring one together, we might have laughed—or cried—depending on the day. Both of us had been through failed marriages, and each of us carried the scars and regrets that come with them. We knew the ache of dashed hopes. We knew what it was like to wake up and realize that what we thought would last forever had slipped through our fingers. For a time, we wondered if we were simply destined to get it wrong. To be honest, our failed marriages caused us to feel as though we were not qualified to write a book on this subject. Instead, our failures taught us valuable lessons, which we are now sharing with you.

But God, in His kindness and mercy, was not finished with us. He began writing a different story—one marked by redemption, grace, and second chances. Through His wisdom and providence, we found each other, and today we enjoy a marriage that is vibrant, joyful, and rooted in trust. That doesn't mean it's perfect. We still make mistakes. We still have disagreements, and regrets about the times we didn't perform to expectations. But over the years, we've learned some beneficial principles—biblical, practical, hard-earned—that have helped us avoid the pitfalls of our past and build something new, solid, and lasting.

We're not offering theories from an ivory tower. What you'll read in these pages comes from two people who have been where you might be right now—disappointed, frustrated, maybe even afraid that the damage is too deep to repair. Or perhaps you're engaged, or newly married, and you want to start strong. Wherever you are on the journey, we want you to know there is hope. God's blueprint for marriage still works, and His wisdom is available to anyone who asks.

This book is our way of passing along what He's taught us: the lessons that came through scripture, the insights that came through prayer, and the perspective that came through failure and healing. We'll share openly about our own missteps—not to dwell on the past, but to show you that even broken beginnings can lead to beautiful endings when God is in the center. Along the way, we'll weave in biblical truth, personal stories, and practical steps you can take to strengthen your marriage starting today.

Our prayer is that as you read, you'll find encouragement where you feel weary, clarity where things have been confusing, and fresh hope for what's ahead. Whether you're building from the ground up or repairing what's been damaged, you can have a marriage that is not just good, but life-giving—one that reflects the heart of God and stands the test of time.

So let's begin.

CHAPTER ONE

The Covenant Foundation

| *Dave's perspective* |

BEFORE WE DISCUSS THE PRACTICAL habits and spiritual principles that can make a marriage thrive, we must start at the beginning. Every lasting structure is built on a foundation that can bear its weight, and marriage is no different. The blueprint God designed is not just old-fashioned wisdom; it's a timeless truth that still holds true in a world that has forgotten where love comes from. In this chapter, we'll explore that foundation—not as a set of rigid rules, but as a living covenant that breathes life into a relationship. Whether you've been married for decades, are just starting out, or are somewhere in between, understanding God's original design will give you the clarity and confidence to build something that will endure.

Every building needs a foundation. It doesn't matter how beautiful the walls are or how carefully the roof is designed—if the base is weak, the whole structure is in danger. Marriage works the same way. You can have all the romance, chemistry, and good intentions in the world, but if your relationship isn't resting on something solid, the storms of life will erode your once strong marriage.

When God designed marriage, He didn't give us a casual arrangement. In the beginning, when He brought Adam and Eve together, He declared, *"For this reason a man shall leave his father and mother and be joined to his wife, and the two shall become one flesh"* (Genesis 2:24). Those weren't just poetic words for a wedding ceremony—they were God's blueprint. In that single sentence, He laid out the principle of leaving, joining, and becoming. It's more than a legal union. It's a spiritual covenant.

That word "covenant" is important. In the Bible, it is not a temporary agreement based on mutual convenience—it's a sacred, binding relationship sealed in God's presence. When we stood before Him on a windswept beach and vowed to love and honor each other, we entered into something far more powerful than a contract. Contracts are designed to protect individual interests. Covenants join two lives together for a shared purpose. A contract says, "If you fail me, I'm free to walk away." A covenant says, "Even after failure, I'm not leaving. We'll work through it together."

Denise and I understand that idea now, but in our earlier marriages, we didn't fully grasp the concept. Looking back, we can see how we treated marriage more like a partnership with performance clauses. We wanted to be happy, and as long as our needs were met, the relationship felt strong. But when disappointment set in, when expectations weren't met, cracks formed. The foundation was not stable, and our former marriages failed. Without realizing it, we had built our lives on shifting sand.

Every marriage will face seasons of strain—financial pressures, misunderstandings, emotional distance, health issues, or outside interference. The question is not whether those seasons will come, but whether the foundation can handle them. When your marriage is built on covenant, those storms don't have the final word. You remember your vows. You lean into God's grace. You fight *for* each other instead of *against* each other.

A covenant also redefines how we see our roles. Too often, the concept of "roles" in marriage has been twisted into something God never intended—where one partner dominates and the other is silenced. But Ephesians chapter five paints a different picture. Paul wrote: *"Submit to one another out of reverence for Christ"* (Ephesians 5:21). Yes, there is headship in the sense of spiritual covering, but it is rooted in sacrificial love, not control. Husbands are called to love their wives *"just as Christ loved the church and gave Himself up for her"* (v. 25). Wives are called to honor and respect their husbands. It's mutual service, each one looking for ways to lift the other higher.

When we begin to see marriage this way—as a living covenant designed for mutual flourishing—it changes everything. Instead of keeping score or fighting for personal gain, we fight to protect what God has joined, and pursue His purposes for our lives. That's why covenant thinking matters. It shifts the focus from "me" to "we," from temporary happiness to long-term faithfulness, from surviving to thriving.

If your marriage is on shaky ground right now, please hear this: God can rebuild any foundation. It will take time. It may require humility and forgiveness you don't feel ready to give. But He is a master builder, and He knows how to take what's broken and make it stronger than before. And if you're starting your marriage journey, this is the time to lay a solid foundation. Choose now to see your vows as more than promises—they are sacred commitments made before God, meant to endure through every season.

We've both learned, sometimes the hard way, that marriage is not just about *finding* the right person—it's about *being* the right person. A covenant isn't kept by feelings alone; it's kept by daily choices to love, honor, forgive, and protect. It's built one day at a time, brick by brick, choice by choice, with God's Word as the blueprint and His Spirit teaching you how to build.

Next, we'll look at the practical ways to protect and strengthen your marriage. But everything we'll share rests on this truth: a covenant marriage is worth fighting for. And it begins with a decision to build on the foundation God designed from the start.

God, the Divine Matchmaker

| *Dave's perspective* |

SOME PEOPLE HAVE A KNACK for choosing the right spouse. They know the qualities they want in a partner, they pick well, and they build a life that lasts. I'm not one of those people. If anything, I had the opposite talent. My track record made it painfully clear that my "picker" was broken. I went for women who were beautiful and charming, but I rarely looked under the hood. Compatibility issues were always there—I just ignored them, hoping they would go away. But they never did. Instead, those differences eventually became irreconcilable and ended the relationship.

Years ago, I found myself newly divorced, and I knew something had to change. I didn't just need a fresh start; I needed a new approach. The first step was admitting that I wasn't qualified to make this decision on my own. I'd been choosing based on my own preferences, and it hadn't worked out. This time, I wanted God's choice.

I joined an online dating platform, started browsing, and soon learned that finding my next wife this way was going to be a slow process. While sifting through hundreds of profiles, reading details, and looking at photos, I was quietly ticking boxes in my head. But I wasn't seeing the qualities I was looking for—someone who believed the Bible, had emotional stability, and, if I were lucky, maybe even a good singing voice. For months, no one caught my eye.

Then I saw her—Denise.

Her profile stood out from the rest. It was detailed, thoughtful, and real. No vague clichés. No shallow self-promotion. Everything she had written checked the boxes I'd been praying about. I sent an inquiry and she replied.

That's when something happened that I hadn't experienced before in the dating process. I distinctly remember the Holy Spirit speaking to my heart: *Trust that she is the right woman. Commit yourself to her completely. Show no signs of indecision or doubt.* I decided to heed the instruction believing that I was hearing God correctly.

We exchanged several emails that first day—short, easy conversations that felt like they'd been waiting to happen. By my third email, I wrote something that was completely out of character for me: *"We should skip the formalities and get married."* I wasn't joking. And although I didn't know it at the time, that statement touched something deep inside Denise's heart.

You see, she had been single for six years after her second divorce. In that time, she'd met men who were happy to "date," but none were willing to commit. Some had been wounded by women in their past and they were afraid of a repeat. Others seemed interested, but they would vanish after a short while, only to pop back into her life months later with no good explanation. She wasn't interested in playing games anymore. My premature proposal may have been unconventional, but it sent a clear message: I was serious.

We began what you might call a long-distance courtship—3,000 miles apart, dating by text, email, and phone calls. (This was before video chat, so we never saw each other's faces in real time.) After three months, I flew to Pennsylvania to meet her in person. Denise introduced me to her family and co-workers, and after a short visit, I flew home to Washington state. By then, we knew we wanted to spend our lives together. We planned a beach wedding three months later, having met in person just once.

That might sound reckless to some people. But here's the thing: when you know you can't trust your own judgment, and you've placed the decision in God's hands, you can have confidence that doesn't come from yourself. This wasn't blind faith—it was trust in the One who sees the end from the beginning.

This principle isn't new. In Genesis 24, when Abraham's servant went to find a wife for Isaac, Isaac abandoned the opportunity to make his own choice. He trusted that the servant, under God's direction, would bring home the right woman. And when Rebekah arrived, Isaac didn't hesitate—he committed to her. Scripture says, *"So she became his wife, and he loved her"* (Genesis 24:67). Notice the order: love followed commitment. Isaac understood that love is not merely an emotion you stumble into; it is a deliberate decision to give yourself fully to another person. That choice created the foundation for their marriage. And it worked out.

One of the little surprises of our marriage was discovering how our preferences lined up in unexpected ways. Denise doesn't enjoy the pressure of planning meals and cooking every day, and I happen to love cooking. She never has to wonder what's for dinner, and I get to relax in the kitchen, which is one of my favorite places to be. We've both learned that God's matchmaking isn't just about big-picture compatibility—it's also about the little details that make life together more enjoyable.

There isn't anything magical about online dating. Our success came when we let go of the need to control the process and allowed God to do what we couldn't. Proverbs 3:5–6 says, *"Trust in the Lord with all your heart and lean not on your own understanding; in all your ways submit to him, and he will make your paths straight."* That's precisely what happened.

If you've struggled to find the right person, or if you're afraid of repeating the mistakes of your past, let our story encourage you. God knows how to bring two people together in a way that makes sense in His timing, even if it doesn't make sense to anyone else. He's the One who can see beyond attraction, beyond finances, into the kind of compatibility that will stand the test of time.

You don't have to rush the process. You don't have to manipulate it. You can let go of fear and trust that the God who designed marriage knows exactly how to put yours together. We're living proof that when you let Him be the matchmaker, you get more than a spouse—you get a partner ideally suited for your life, your calling, and your future.

CHAPTER THREE

Compatibility

| *Dave's perspective* |

THE WORD COMPATIBILITY GETS TOSSED around a lot in dating communities, but it's often misunderstood. People talk about having "chemistry" or "common interests," and those things can be important. But when we're talking about a lifelong covenant, compatibility goes much deeper. It's not just about whether you both enjoy hiking or can quote lines from the same movies. Relational compatibility means your values, goals, and needs fit together in a way that will stand the test of time.

We've both learned—through hard experience—that ignoring compatibility issues doesn't make them disappear. In our earlier marriages, there were things we knew deep down that didn't align, but we convinced ourselves that love would overcome them, or that the other person would eventually change. That's a dangerous gamble. Love can cover many faults, but it doesn't erase fundamental differences in values, faith, or emotional maturity. And there is never a guarantee that someone will change. Those differences eventually show up, and when they do, they can shake the relationship to its core.

That's one reason our story is different. Our previous relationship failures helped us develop an understanding of the traits that were most important to us in a potential life partner. I wanted a Bible-believing, emotionally stable woman, and Denise was looking for a Godly man who would commit to a long-term marriage. Neither of us was seeking perfection, but we wanted alignment in the things that mattered most. If you haven't had previous relationships that inform you of what matters most to you in marriage, it might be helpful to think deeply about these things and even make a list of traits you admire in other successful couples.

Compatibility begins with shared beliefs. The bible is clear on this point: *"Can two walk together unless they are agreed?"* (Amos 3:3). When a couple doesn't share the same spiritual foundation, it affects everything—how you make decisions, how you handle conflict, how you raise children, and how you face trials. Faith shapes your worldview, your priorities, and even your sense of purpose. Without alignment on these issues, the road ahead will be rocky.

Another layer of compatibility is emotional health. Everyone has wounds from the past, but not everyone has dealt with them. Emotional instability—whether it shows up as volatility, withdrawal, or unresolved trauma—can create behavioral patterns that are exhausting to live with. Part of choosing a partner wisely is paying attention to how they handle disappointment, stress, and conflict. Do they communicate honestly? Do they take responsibility for their actions? Can they manage their emotions without lashing out or shutting down? These are questions worth asking, because marriage has a way of magnifying, not minimizing, our personal strengths and weaknesses.

Then there's the everyday rhythm of life. You don't have to be alike in everything—I prefer silence when I'm working, and Denise likes to listen to podcasts—but you do need to find a harmony in how you approach daily living. Things like money management, work ethic, family expectations, and even how you spend your downtime may not seem critical early on, but over years of marriage, they can either create peace or constant tension. Compatibility means you can live in the same space, work toward the same goals, and enjoy moving in the same direction in life without feeling like you're constantly pulling against each other.

No couple is perfectly compatible. Everyone brings personal differences into a marriage, and navigating those differences can become a source of growth. But the key is knowing which differences you can work with and which will cause ongoing friction. It's essential to spend time getting to know each other before making a lifelong commitment. Listen carefully to what the other person says about their dreams, struggles, faith, and relationships with family and friends. Pay attention to what they *do*, not just what they *say*. Time has a way of revealing whether the connection is deep enough to last.

When we met, we were 3,000 miles apart, but our long-distance conversations gave us the chance to ask the right questions. We talked about faith, family, finances, and the kind of life we wanted to build. We were honest about our past failures and what we'd learned from them. By the time we met in person, we already knew that our hearts and values were in sync. That didn't mean we wouldn't face challenges, but it meant we'd be facing them from the same side of the battlefield.

If you're married and have discovered that compatibility is a struggle, take heart—it's not hopeless. You may need to have some honest—and possibly difficult—conversations about your differences. You may want to seek counseling or bring a trusted mentor into the conversation. But even in cases where alignment wasn't there at the start, God has a way of drawing two hearts closer when both people are willing to submit to Him.

Marriage isn't about finding a partner who matches you in every detail— it's about finding someone who shares your deepest commitments and is willing to grow with you in the rest. Compatibility is the soil where the seeds of love, respect, and partnership can take root. Without it, marriage is a constant struggle. With it, the work of marriage becomes a joy, because you're creating something together that neither of you could build alone.

CHAPTER FOUR

Becoming the Right Person

| *Dave's perspective* |

AFTER I WAS SEPARATED FROM my first wife, I rented a house in Tacoma, Washington, to be closer to work. It happened that the house I rented had cable TV—a luxury I gave up in 1996. Somehow, I became addicted to watching the Food Network. I had always been interested in cooking, though I'd had no formal training. I didn't just watch for entertainment. I learned the techniques of famous chefs and began trying out their recipes. Before long, I was creating sophisticated dishes and launched a cooking blog that featured my favorite recipes.

When I created my profile for an online dating site, I mentioned that I love cooking. I had no idea that this detail was the bait that would help me land my future wife. As it turned out, Denise did not enjoy cooking. She found it stressful. My love for cooking checked a box on her ideal husband list. There's an important principle illustrated in this story that I'd like to unpack.

My decision to learn how to cook was a step that I took to improve myself. I did not specifically aim to make myself a better potential husband, but that was the unintended effect it had. By learning to cook, I made myself appealing to women who might not have otherwise found me quite so desirable.

For several years prior to this, I had spent countless hours listening to sermons from Bible-teaching pastors and conducting my own study of Scripture. I didn't do this to make myself a better potential husband, but again, that was the effect it had. Denise was attracted to me, partly because of my knowledge of the Bible.

We all want a mate who has the qualities we desire. But it's fair to ask: in what ways do we fulfill their desires?

In what ways have we prepared ourselves to be the ideal spouse?

One of the most important lessons we've learned is that it's not a matter of finding the right person—it's more about becoming the right person. That little shift in perspective changes everything.

When people discuss marriage, the conversation almost always centers on compatibility. Compatibility isn't primarily about finding someone who fits your preferences—it's about becoming someone who can love well, forgive often, and serve others.

When Denise and I think about our own story, we sometimes wonder what would have happened if we had met twenty-five years earlier. The answer is simple: it wouldn't have worked out. We weren't ready for each other. We were too immature, too self-focused, and too blind to the things that matter in marriage. Back then, our brokenness and our blind spots would have driven us apart. But life, as hard as it was, gave us the chance to learn and grow. Through failed marriages and painful lessons, we both had to do the work of facing our flaws, healing from our wounds, and allowing God to reshape us. Along the way, we acquired some life skills that we would later need.

By the time we met, we were no longer the same people we had been decades earlier. We had learned how to listen, how to compromise, how to let go of our pride, and how to put Christ at the center. Denise has designed a beautiful home, and she keeps it clean. I'm skilled at most home maintenance jobs. The work we've done to improve ourselves is precisely what makes us compatible.

The healthiest marriages aren't built when perfect people find each other. They're built when two imperfect people are willing to learn and grow. So if you're single and longing to meet the right person, don't just wait around for them to appear. Use your time to become the best version of yourself. Let God heal the parts of you that are still carrying pain. Invite Him to strengthen the areas where you're weak. Ask Him to grow in you the kind of love, patience, and resilience that marriage will require. Learning a few life skills will also help.

If you're already married, this principle still applies. The temptation is to focus on your spouse's shortcomings—if only they would change, things would be better. But the greatest gift you can give your marriage is your own transformation. When you allow God to upgrade you, it not only blesses you—it improves your marriage. We don't stumble into compatibility by luck; it's cultivated as we allow God to shape us into the person He envisioned us to be before we were born.

So whether you're waiting for a spouse, working through challenges in your current marriage, or simply longing for deeper intimacy, start here: become a new person. Let God make you whole. Let Him prepare you for the partnership He has in mind. And when the time is right, you'll discover that the person He brings into your life doesn't complete you—they complement the work He has already done in you.

CHAPTER FIVE

Dating Wisely

| *Denise's perspective* |

WHEN I WAS IN MY 20s and 30s, I didn't take the most active role in choosing who to date. I was generally too passive, and it seemed like I was always waiting for someone to pick me. In hindsight, I believe this stemmed from a lack of self-worth. I was, however, able to dodge some bullets by rejecting those men who were obviously unstable. Even though I tried to be selective about who I allowed into my life, I also overlooked some red flags—rushing into dating and marriage with the idea of living "happily ever after" was beyond foolish. It didn't help that I was an unbeliever at the time and had no biblical instruction or role models.

Failing twice at marriage helped me see that I was really missing something. Thankfully, I accepted Christ as my Savior and asked Him to lead me in my next steps. I realized that committing to someone who *said* they loved me was not a plan if we didn't share the same values.

I wanted to learn what God said about relationships and marriage to avoid repeating my past mistakes.

By the time I met Dave, I had been single for six years. During those years, I found a church family, but more importantly, I searched for teaching books with biblical advice on relationships. Wanting to move forward because I still believed in marriage, I found dating to be difficult and discouraging. Were all the good men already taken? Those who were divorced and available had issues that prevented them from being a match for me. I was looking for someone who was committed to building a life together based on shared beliefs and goals.

When Dave and I connected online, we were on opposite ends of the country. At first, that distance might seem like an obstacle, but I see now it was a gift. Long-distance dating removes a lot of the distractions that come with dating in person. It takes the focus off physical attraction and eliminates the temptation to cross physical boundaries. Without those pressures, we had space to get to know each other's minds and hearts. We weren't building a relationship on how much we liked each other's smile or how fun our Friday nights were. We were building it on something deeper.

Instead of typical dates, we listened to audio messages and read books about marriage. Then we'd get on the phone and talk about what we'd learned—what stood out to us, what made us stop and think, and how the ideas connected to our own stories. We discussed the root causes of our past relationship problems and, more importantly, how to avoid repeating them. Those conversations forced us to be vulnerable, but they were also rich with hope.

Our dating process wasn't about trying to impress each other with surface qualities; we knew we had to get into heavier issues. It was about learning how to be the best spouse we could be—not just for our own future happiness, but for the sake of the other person. We were each asking, *"How can I love and serve this person well if we do get married?"* That's a very different question from, *"What can this person do for me?"*

That intentional focus set us up for the kind of marriage we have today. We weren't distracted by short-term thrills; we were laying a long-term foundation. Proverbs 24:3 says, *"By wisdom a house is built, and through understanding it is established."* That's what we were doing, even if we didn't fully realize it at the time.

Because we never really *dated* in person before we married—just one short in-person visit before the wedding—we decided that after we were married, we would make up for lost time in a way that would strengthen our bond. So we started a weekly date night tradition. Every week, no matter how busy life gets, we set aside time to focus on each other. We just celebrated our eighteenth anniversary, and that tradition is still going strong. Those evenings remind us that dating isn't something you leave behind after you say "I do." It's something you carry into marriage to keep the connection alive.

If you are dating with the goal of finding a Godly spouse, use that time to ask questions that help you get to know the values, faith, and goals of that person. Of course, you'll want to also observe their actions in different situations—with their family, with your family, and friends. Do they treat people with respect? Do they have a life of faith—and is it compatible with yours? Spend enough time to sense if they're merely telling you what you want to hear, or if they're genuine. Some people marry and find out *later* that their spouse doesn't want children. Don't get too attached to the person if they're not in alignment with your core values. I learned this the hard way. Some things should be deal breakers—especially if you don't align on the big things, such as faith, children, finances, and life goals. Political views might also be important.

For us, dating was never just about finding someone we enjoyed spending time with—it was about preparing ourselves to walk together in covenant. And in that sense, our long-distance courtship was precisely what we needed. It may not be for everyone, but it gave us the space, focus, time to talk, and intentionality to build something that has lasted far beyond the wedding day.

Note: For some people, searching for a compatible person online opens up a larger field of potential partners—especially if they don't have much contact with others in their day-to-day life. Of course, most people understand there are certain dangers when meeting people online.

If you aren't aware, please educate yourself to avoid common pitfalls. Precautions should always be taken to lessen the risks.

For example:

Share information about who you're meeting online with someone you trust in real life; they may be able to spot issues that you don't see.

Do your research. Seriously, there are websites where you can look up information on an individual to see if there's any relevant history that you should know. Sometimes you only need a name or email address, and perhaps their age, to get a search started.

Be patient—don't rush into a date with them right away.

If you go on a date, always make sure someone you trust knows when and where you're going.

Date in a public place, such as a restaurant or coffee shop.

Have an emergency plan to get yourself out of the date in case something goes wrong.

If you're discerning—able to differentiate sincerity from deception—it *is* possible to meet someone online who shares your beliefs. Be honest about what you want and expect. Get to know them from a distance first. Build trust. Ask for insight from the Lord.

CHAPTER SIX

Radical Transparency

| *Dave's perspective* |

TRUST IS ONE OF THOSE things that everyone knows is important, but not everyone knows how to build. We tend to think of trust as something that happens over time—if you spend enough time together, trust will naturally appear. But that's not how it works. Trust doesn't grow by accident. It's built on purpose, choice by choice, through the way we treat each other and the way in which we handle relational difficulties.

For us, trust didn't start with a wedding ring. It began long before we ever met in person. Because our relationship began long-distance, we had no choice but to build it on words. As we said, there were no distractions coming from physical temptation or the typical dating scene. Instead, we filled our days with emails, phone calls, and long conversations about who we were, what we'd been through, and what we wanted for the future.

We learned each other's values, hopes, and even our shortcomings through the books we read together and the audio messages we discussed. That honesty created a foundation for something much more profound than a romance—it created a sense of safety.

One of the most significant turning points in building trust came with our decision to practice radical transparency. I had a long talk with Denise where I told her everything—my failures, my weaknesses, the jobs I'd been fired from, the reasons for my divorce—every detail that I might have been tempted to hide. She listened, processed, and accepted me as I was, noting that I had learned some hard lessons and was making changes with God's help. A week later, she did the same for me. She bared her soul, and I stayed. Those conversations left no room for hidden landmines to explode later. We knew exactly who we were marrying, scars and all.

Trusting one another before marriage is more than proving you won't betray each other—it's showing you can handle each other's imperfections without overreacting. It requires taking risks and working to create an atmosphere where fears, doubts, and flaws can be shared and discussed calmly. I encourage you to bring your authentic self to the relationship and trust God with the outcome. When trust is intentionally built before the wedding, it changes how you approach marriage. You're not carrying secret fears about what might surface later. You're not wondering if the other person is holding something back. You're free to focus on building a life together, not unraveling mysteries from the past.

That's not to say trust is a one-time achievement. Trust isn't automatic. It's earned, nurtured, and protected. Even in marriage, it's something you keep building. That's why we made date night a weekly tradition from the very beginning. We've kept it up for eighteen years. It's not just about going out to dinner—it's about staying connected, keeping the lines of communication open, and continuing to invest in the relationship we started with such intentional care.

When you commit to being honest and open at the start of your relationship, you give your marriage a head start that will carry you through the challenges ahead. For us, it was worth every long conversation, every vulnerable moment, and every honest answer. It's the reason we were able to start our life together on solid ground.

But here's something we've noticed over the years: many people walk into dating—or even into marriage—already carrying wounds from the past. They've been ignored, belittled, abused, treated unkindly, or betrayed. Sometimes it was in childhood; sometimes in a previous relationship. And those wounds don't disappear when a new relationship begins.

A wounded soul finds it difficult to trust others, even when the other person has done nothing to deserve suspicion. The result is often a cycle—pulling away before you can be hurt again, building walls to keep people out, or clinging too tightly out of fear they'll leave. And when those wounds are joined to the lingering emotional bonds from past relationships—what scripture calls "soul ties"—they can complicate dating and marriage in ways many couples don't fully understand.

That's why it's best to address these issues up front, before they have the chance to sabotage what could be a beautiful relationship. Healing soul wounds and breaking unhealthy ties from the past will position you for success, giving you the freedom to trust and be trusted.

In the next chapter, we'll discuss what soul wounds and soul ties are, how they're formed, and how they affect marriage—along with practical ways to bring them to God for healing and freedom.

The Effects of Soul Wounds and Soul Ties

| *Denise's perspective* |

IF YOU'VE EVER STRUGGLED TO trust someone you genuinely wanted to trust, you already know how powerful the past can be. We don't start relationships as blank slates—we carry with us the experiences, good and bad, that have shaped us along the way. Some of those experiences leave wounds that run deeper than we realize, and those wounds can complicate relationships.

Soul wounds happen when our heart, mind, or emotions have been injured. Sometimes they form in childhood, from a parent's neglect or harsh words. Other times, they come from past romantic relationships—betrayal, rejection, manipulation, or abuse. When someone you trust ignores, belittles, or abandons you, it leaves a lasting mark. Those wounds don't just fade with time. They lie under the surface, ready to be touched off by the smallest reminder of past pain. They must be brought to God for healing.

That's why some people have what we call "trust issues." It's not that they don't want to trust; it's that their soul has learned, sometimes the hard way, that trusting can lead to hurt. So they protect themselves—by keeping their guard up, pulling away before things get too close, or questioning the motives of someone who's actually trying to love them.

When you add *soul ties* to the mix, things get even more complicated.

A soul tie is an emotional or spiritual bond between two people. God designed soul ties to be good—bonds formed in covenant relationships, like marriage, or in healthy, godly friendships. The Bible says of David and Jonathan, *"the soul of Jonathan was knit to the soul of David"* (1 Samuel 18:1). That's a godly soul tie, built on loyalty and love.

But soul ties can also be unhealthy. Romantic or sexual relationships outside of marriage can form deep emotional and spiritual bonds that linger long after the relationship has ended. Abusive relationships can create unhealthy attachments where a person feels drawn back to the very one who harmed them. These bonds can carry emotional baggage—such as unresolved longing, anger, bitterness, and shame—straight into the next relationship.

In marriage, unhealed wounds and unbroken soul ties can show up in subtle ways. A spouse may overreact to something minor because it reminds them of a past betrayal. They may compare their spouse to someone from their past, consciously or not. In some cases, they may even feel guilty for loving their spouse because part of their heart is still bound to someone else. None of this means the marriage is doomed—it means there's work to be done in the soul.

Dave and I knew we wanted to start our marriage with as few hidden obstacles as possible. That's why we chose radical transparency during our engagement. But even with that honesty, both of us had to bring our past wounds and unhealthy attachments before God for healing. We didn't want to spend our early years together fighting battles from someone else's war.

If you want a healthy marriage, the time to deal with these issues is before the wedding—though it's never too late. Start by asking God to show you where the pain points are. Who has hurt you in a way that still affects how you trust today? Are there relationships from your past where your heart is still entangled? Do memories of certain people or events still stir strong emotions—anger, longing, resentment—that don't belong in your present?

When God reveals a soul wound, invite Him into that memory. Let Him show you where He was in the moment you were hurt. Forgive the one who wronged you, even if you never hear an apology. Forgiveness doesn't excuse their behavior; it frees you from its grip. Then, ask God to remove the painful emotion.

When God reveals an unhealthy soul tie, renounce [disavow, disown, deny] it in prayer. Break the bond in Jesus' name, and ask Him to sever every connection that keeps your heart tied to the past. Replace that connection with a fresh commitment to the person God has given you now—or, if you're not yet married, to the spouse He will one day bring.

Healing soul wounds and breaking unhealthy soul ties isn't just about cleaning up the past—it's about protecting your future. It positions you to love without fear, trust without hesitation, and give yourself fully to the present relationship. It keeps yesterday's pain from stealing tomorrow's joy.

In the next chapter, we're going to look at what we call *The Four Laws of Marriage*. These aren't legalistic rules; they're God-given principles that protect and strengthen the covenant you've made. When they're in place, they help guard against the very wounds and entanglements we've been discussing, making your marriage a safe and thriving environment for both of you.

CHAPTER EIGHT

The Four Laws of Marriage

| *Dave's perspective* |

MARRIAGE IS NOT MEANT TO be a guessing game. God didn't bring Adam and Eve together, wish them luck, and then step back to see if they could figure it out on their own. He wanted them to succeed, so He set in place certain principles—laws, you might say—that, when they are followed, make marriage work. These aren't laws in the sense of rigid rules that you must follow to earn God's approval. They're like the laws of gravity and thermodynamics; they work whether you believe in them or not, and when you follow them, your marriage will benefit. When you read them, you will probably recognize the common-sense quality in these foundational ideas.

These four laws come from Genesis 2:24: *"For this reason a man shall leave his father and mother and be joined to his wife, and they shall become one flesh."* In that one sentence, God lays out a blueprint that still works today. Some call them "The Four Laws of Marriage," and over the years, we've found them to be as true now as they were in the Garden of Eden.

Law #1: Prioritize Your Spouse – Leave

The first thing God says is that a man will leave his father and mother. That's not a call to cut ties or stop honoring your parents—it's about shifting the primary human relationship in your life. Once you marry, your spouse becomes your number one priority on this earth.

In practice, that means your spouse comes before your parents, friends, career, hobbies, and *even your children*. As precious as your children are, if the marriage becomes unstable, the children's future also becomes unstable. Therefore, guarding time together and making decisions that protect your marriage is critical. We've seen many marriages struggle because one spouse never entirely left their old loyalties. Sometimes it's a parent who still holds too much sway, or friends who get more emotional energy than the marriage does. Prioritizing each other isn't selfish—it's the way God designed marriage to work.

Law #2: Pursue Your Spouse – Be joined

The second part of the verse says the man will be joined to his wife. Some translations say "cleave," which paints the picture of holding on tightly. In other words, you don't just win your spouse's heart once and then coast. You keep pursuing them.

When we were dating long-distance, pursuing each other was natural—we talked constantly, sent emails, and couldn't wait for the next call. But after marriage, life has a way of filling up with responsibilities. If we're not intentional, the relationship can slide into a rut. That's one reason we committed to a weekly date night from the start. We go out together once a week—usually it's for dinner, but it could even be taking a long drive in the Jeep at sunset. For eighteen years, that's been our way of saying, "You still matter most to me." Pursuit doesn't have to be grand gestures—it's the daily and weekly choices to connect, encourage, and show affection.

Law #3: Maintain Purity – Be one flesh

Becoming "one flesh" is about unity in every part of life. That unity can't thrive if outside influences are polluting the relationship. Purity means protecting your marriage from anything that would divide your hearts—pornography, emotional affairs, flirting, secret friendships, even unchecked resentment.

Purity is also about transparency. It's easier to maintain purity when you commit to living transparently. We don't hide passwords, purchases, or private conversations. Purity is easier to maintain when you establish deliberate practices to live in the light with one another.

Law #4: Practice Permanence – They shall become one flesh

The fourth law is embedded in the whole verse; God intended marriage to be a lifelong covenant. It's not a trial run or a contract with escape clauses—it's a vow to love, honor, and remain faithful "for better or worse" for the rest of your lives.

When permanence is your mindset, you stop looking for a way out and start looking for a way through. Challenges become opportunities to work together, not reasons to separate. It's a commitment that says, "We may fight, we may hurt, but we're going to make it right—because we're in this for the long haul."

These four laws work together. Prioritizing your spouse creates security. Pursuing them over the long haul keeps love alive. Maintaining purity protects trust. Practicing permanence builds resilience. Ignore them, and the marriage will eventually weaken. Live by them, and you'll have a foundation strong enough to weather anything life throws your way.

Marriage may be complex at times, but God's blueprint is simple—and it works. The same wisdom He gave Adam and Eve still holds true today. If you build your marriage on these four principles, you're not just following good advice; you're aligning with the way God designed love to last.

Generational Issues

| *Denise's perspective* |

ONE OF THE MOST DAUNTING realizations in marriage is that we don't just bring ourselves into the relationship—we bring our families with us. Not in a literal sense, of course, but in the patterns, beliefs, and ways of relating that were passed down to us, sometimes without our even noticing.

Some of those patterns are desirable. Maybe you grew up in a home where kindness was the norm, where hard work was valued, or where prayer was as natural as breathing. Those are gifts you can pass along to your spouse and children. But not every inheritance is good. Some of us carry patterns and poor coping behaviors we'd rather not pass on—things like anger, addiction, manipulation, dishonesty, divorce, abuse, or fear. These things can weave themselves into the fabric of a family so tightly that they feel "normal," even though they've been damaging generation after generation.

The Bible talks about this reality in sobering terms. In Exodus 20:5–6, God warns that the sins of the fathers can affect the children to the third and fourth generation, but He also promises to show mercy to a thousand generations of those who love Him and keep His commands. That's the hope we hold onto—no matter what's been handed down to us, God's mercy is more powerful. He can break destructive cycles and start new legacies of blessing.

The first step is recognizing inherited patterns. Take an honest look at your family history. Are there recurring struggles in relationships? Are there patterns of infidelity, control, substance abuse, or mental instability? Do you see cycles of poverty, broken trust, or violence? These patterns aren't coincidences—they often point to what scripture calls "generational iniquity." Sometimes they're learned behaviors. Sometimes, they're the lingering influence of spiritual strongholds passed down through the family line.

When Dave and I looked at our family histories, we could see certain patterns that had been repeated. Some were obvious; others became clear only when we compared stories and noticed similarities. We realized that if we didn't address them, we might end up carrying those same unhealthy dynamics into our marriage. We also knew we didn't want to pass them on to the next generation.

Breaking generational curses is not about blaming your parents or grandparents. They likely inherited their own struggles and did the best they could with what they knew. Breaking a curse is taking responsibility for what you carry now, so it loses its power over you and your family.

The process begins with repentance, even if you weren't the one who started it. You can stand before God on behalf of your family line and say, "Lord, I confess the sins that have been in my family—whether it's anger, abuse, dishonesty, sexual immorality, addiction, or anything else that You reveal to me. I repent for these sins, and I ask You to cleanse me and my family by the blood of Jesus."

Repentance can be defined as changing one's old way of thinking, turning away from past wrongdoing, and seeking God's ways.

From there, you renounce [disavow, disown, deny] the enemy's right to continue that pattern in your life. You declare that the curse is broken and that you will not participate in it any longer. You replace it with the truth of God's Word, speaking blessing and life over your marriage and children. Galatians 3:13 reminds us that *"Christ redeemed us from the curse of the law by becoming a curse for us."* His death and resurrection have already paid the price; our part is to agree with that victory and walk in it.

Once you've addressed the spiritual side, be intentional about the practical side. If your family has struggled with poor communication, learn healthy ways to discuss and resolve conflicts. If there's a history of addiction, set boundaries around situations that could draw you in. If finances were always chaotic, build habits of wise stewardship together. Breaking a curse is not just a one-time prayer—it's a new way of living, step by step.

When you and your spouse face generational issues together, it strengthens your bond. You're not blaming each other for your pasts—you're linking arms to fight for your future. You're choosing to pass on blessings instead of burdens. And in doing so, you're investing in the generations to come.

Your marriage can be the point where the old cycle ends and a new one begins. You may have inherited patterns you didn't choose, but you have the power, in Christ, to determine what gets passed on from here. That's the beauty of being rescued from the past to live the life God intended—this redemption doesn't just change you, it changes the whole family line.

CHAPTER TEN

His Needs, Her Needs — Kingdom Style

| *Dave's perspective* |

IN THE FIRST YEAR OF our marriage, Denise and I explored the idea of creating a ministry for struggling couples. We thought we might host marriage workshops to provide other couples with tools to stay together so they could avoid the pain and suffering we experienced in our past. We enrolled in a class that would teach us how to facilitate these kinds of events.

One of the required books for the class was *His Needs, Her Needs* by Willard Harley. It's a well-known book in marriage counseling circles, but at the time, I had no idea how deeply it would impact us.

The class had a unique exercise. Men were given blue highlighters, women were given pink ones. The instructions were simple: read each chapter on your own, highlighting anything you wanted your spouse to notice. Then, read the same chapter together, focusing on what the other person had highlighted. The bonus came when you saw that both of you had highlighted the same section—those were moments of instant clarity, where the "aha" was shared.

When I got to the chapter on emotional needs in the book, it hit me like a ton of bricks. I didn't even know I had emotional needs. But as I read and reflected, it became painfully clear why my first marriage had failed. I hadn't been meeting my ex-wife's emotional needs, and she hadn't been meeting mine. So we each turned to other people—friends, acquaintances—who would meet those needs in ways our marriage no longer did. Without realizing it, we drifted apart physically, emotionally, and spiritually until there was nothing left holding us together.

That realization was a turning point for me. I understood that meeting each other's emotional needs wasn't a bonus or a luxury—it was essential for the survival and health of a marriage. Denise and I decided that this would become one of the foundational blocks of our relationship.

Men's Needs—General Tendencies

In general (though not always), men and women differ in the way they prioritize certain needs. In our workshop, we were surprised to learn that first, men need ***respect***. If respect is not there, a man will struggle to thrive in the relationship. The Bible in various places instructs wives to respect to their husbands. It seems God knows about this emotional need. Most people believe men value sexual fulfillment first, but it seemed to rank second in our studies. However, it *is* an important need that creates a special bond in marriage, and should be treated as such. Men also need recreational companionship—doing enjoyable activities with their spouse. They may have a lower need for long, emotionally deep conversations or hobbies like gardening.

If top needs are not met, things can go sideways. If a wife is disrespectful to her husband—giving him glances of disapproval, complaining about or insulting him, especially in front of family and friends—it is destructive. We witnessed an example of this in a couple we knew. The husband was beaten down and devalued. Denise tried to counsel the wife about it. She didn't take the advice, and we saw the behavior continue until they moved out of state.

Denise has a strong position against the epidemic of disrespect, notably towards men, which has risen in the last decade, maybe longer. If our Western society could reject this attitude of disrespect, she believes society would rapidly sort out many other problems. Men and women should work for, not against each other, in marriage. Disrespect can gradually divide them and erode the feelings of companionship and love that were once strong.

Despite the potential difficulties today's couples face, there's always hope if we're willing to submit to a process of change. Marriages on the brink of destruction can turn around. It can happen even when only one partner changes their behavior towards their spouse. It doesn't have to require years of marriage counseling if one spouse can start the process of change. Of course, it's best if both husband and wife make changes together, but sometimes the wife will adjust her attitude, and the husband will follow. He will react positively to the new behavior or attitude she's projecting toward him. We've seen this happen—it transformed a marriage in which the wife was about to move out of the home. Of course, it can also work similarly if the husband takes the initiative to make changes first.

Women's Needs—General Tendencies

Women, on the other hand, often prioritize *security* in every area—in their relationships, with their children, their finances, and their households. Women also tend to value emotional connection, meaningful conversation, and quality time—while their need for sex, in terms of frequency or urgency, may be lower. Of course, there are exceptions, and some couples are wired in reverse. But the point is this: if those differences are not recognized and addressed, they will become friction points in the marriage.

A wife who craves conversation and emotional closeness yet marries a man who has little interest in communication might develop an "emotional affair" with a co-worker, sharing her thoughts, fears, and victories with him instead of with her husband. When her spouse finds out, the betrayal feels every bit as real as a physical affair. And let's face it, an emotional connection can sometimes lead to a physical affair. Those who address the top needs of their spouse can avoid this destructive outcome for the marriage and the family.

The Cost of Meeting Needs

Meeting each other's emotional needs often requires sacrifice. For most women, security is a top priority. Security isn't just financial stability—it's the assurance that her husband is safe, healthy, and not putting himself in unnecessary danger.

When Denise and I worked through our emotional needs inventory, it became evident to me that my high-risk hobbies—mountaineering, kayaking, rock climbing—were a problem for her. One example stands out: I had always wanted to climb Mount Rainier. But for Denise, the thought of me being on that mountain was a nightmare. She pictured crevasses, sudden storms, and me not coming home. For her, the anxiety was too much. Security was non-negotiable. So I gave it up. Not grudgingly, but willingly—because I wanted her to feel safe in our marriage. As it turned out, when we took a recreational interest inventory, we found we both enjoyed golf. That became our shared activity. I gave up a dangerous hobby, and in return, I got something that brought us closer together.

To Denise, I met another need by having what she calls "a teachable spirit." She wanted a lifelong learner, not someone who felt he had life all figured out. We gradually gave up some rigid church doctrines, and I became open to a new church she wanted to explore. We learned about the prophetic, and as I stepped into my role as the spiritual leader of the household, I met another need she had.

Denise has made sacrifices for me, too. She is famous for reminding me that she didn't move across the country, leave her family, her friends, her job, and sell her home in Pennsylvania to have her new husband die on a mountaintop, all for the thrill of it. She loves me, and is rightly protective—not just for the sake of *her* security, but for the stability of our blended family as well. She adjusted her habits to accommodate my unusual paramedic work schedule. She started a freelance graphic design business from home until she found a regular job in the area. She endured the dark, cloudy, rainy weather of the Pacific Northwest even though she craved sunshine and warmth. That's the essence of covenant love: putting the needs of your spouse ahead of your own, not because you're keeping score, but because you value the relationship more than your comfort.

In John 15:13, Jesus said, *"Greater love has no one than this: to lay down one's life for one's friends."* In marriage, that "laying down" happens in daily choices—meeting your spouse's needs even when it costs you something.

Independent Behavior

When you first hear the phrase *independent behavior,* it might sound positive. In American culture, independence is often equated with liberty, and the freedom to chart one's own destiny. But in marriage, independent behavior is the tendency to act independently of your spouse's needs, without their participation, and often without their knowledge. We learned of this term from a second book we read for our marriage facilitators workshop—*Love Busters,* also by Willard Harley. The key principle was the idea that married people should not act like they did when they were single.

Particular examples of independent behavior may seem harmless, such as spending every Friday night socializing with friends from the office after work. It may have been customary to have a "girl's night out" when you weren't married, but your husband doesn't fit in. Or maybe you went bowling on certain nights, without fail, and followed up with drinks or food with your buddies afterwards. Your wife doesn't enjoy bowling, and she's starting to feel neglected.

Other examples include keeping an old email address or social media account that a previous admirer used to contact you. These behaviors create insecurity for your spouse and could lead to trouble if it appears you are secretly trying to keep access open to a past relationship.

Then, there are *extremely* independent behaviors that are intentionally deceptive, such as having a secret bank account, engaging in hidden gambling, or making large purchases without agreement on spending with your spouse. In all things, it's best for couples to mutually agree on some ground rules at the start. Discussing your time expenditure and activities can help you come to an agreement that works for both of you.

Transparency as a Remedy

One of the most effective ways to guard against independent behavior is transparency. In our marriage, Denise and I share the passwords and PINs to our electronic devices and social media accounts. At any time, we both know we have access to all devices and online activity. That accountability keeps us honest, but more importantly, it brings peace of mind. Transparency says, *"I have nothing to hide from you, and I'm willing to let you see every part of my life."* That level of openness may feel risky, but it builds trust and removes the breeding ground for secrecy.

A happy marriage doesn't happen by accident. It's built on the intentional meeting of each other's deepest needs, and on the commitment to remove anything—secrecy, neglect, independent behavior—that threatens that connection. When you both strive to live this way, you create a safe, thriving place where love can grow year after year. Instead of *independent behavior,* a more promising alternative is *interdependence* in marriage, where both partners maintain their individuality and also rely on each other for emotional support and connection. This balance allows for mutual respect. It includes healthy boundaries and the ability to grow both in the marriage and as individuals. And that's worth every sacrifice you'll ever make.

Exercise: Meeting Each Other's Emotional Needs

Below is a list of common emotional needs in marriage. As you read through them, I encourage you and your spouse to:
- Review the list together.
- Circle the three needs that matter most to you personally.

- Share with your spouse what "meeting that need" looks like in practical terms.
- Commit to one small action this week to honor your spouse's top need.

This exercise isn't about pointing out what your spouse isn't doing—it's about providing a clear roadmap for how to love each other more effectively.

A List of Emotional Needs in Marriage

Intimate Conversation – More than small talk, this is about open, honest dialogue where both partners feel heard and valued.

Recreational Companionship – Sharing fun activities together builds connection.

Physical Attractiveness – We all want to feel desired by our spouse.

Honesty and Openness – Trust grows when both partners live transparently.

Financial Support – Money can be one of the top struggles in marriage and is often a significant cause of conflict between husband and wife.

Domestic Support – A home doesn't run itself. Sharing responsibilities—meals, laundry, errands, or maintenance—communicates partnership.

Family Commitment – Children, parents, and extended family all impact a marriage.

Affection – Expressing love through touch, words, and gestures of care creates warmth.

Respect – Every person needs to feel that their voice matters.

Admiration – Everyone thrives under encouragement.

Sexual Fulfillment – Intimacy is God's gift for marriage.

Security – A marriage should feel safe, stable, and dependable.

Spiritual Intimacy – Praying together, worshiping together, or encouraging one another in faith strengthens the foundation of your marriage.

Appreciation – Everyone wants to be noticed with words of thanks.

Space/Autonomy – Healthy marriages also respect individuality.

CHAPTER ELEVEN

New Habits

| *Denise's perspective* |

MY LOVING MOTHER DID HER best to meet the family's needs. She was wise in many ways—outgoing, savvy in business, motivated, and full of common sense—but she had a habit that quietly sabotaged her marriage to my father. Disrespect. It wasn't always what she said—it was how she said it. Sometimes, she treated him like a child who needed training. I've seen other women do this as well—they take the role of mother instead of wife and partner. I don't think my mom even realized she did this.

My dad was always the strong, silent type, but I doubt that it was God's plan for him always to take a back seat to her dominance. My handsome and skilled dad became increasingly passive in the relationship and struggled to gain traction in family decision-making. He was the man who worked long hours in the heat of summer and the stinging cold of winter, stacked the hay in the barn loft, and fixed mechanical things. He often seemed exhausted from his physical work. I don't think he ever received any encouragement for all this. He worked hard to provide for us, but he became uninspired in his role as a husband. Looking back, I wish my parents had known more about how to uplift each other as partners. My mom tended to react, and my dad's nature was to retreat.

It wasn't until years later, after reading several books on marriage, that I realized just how deeply most men need respect from the woman they love. For many men, respect is not a luxury—it's as vital to them as communication is to most women. And here's the hard truth: that respect has to be shown even when it isn't "deserved." Perhaps, I should say, even *before* it is "deserved."

I'll be the first to admit that it can be hard. But how can a man step up to a new and bigger role if he's emotionally demeaned at the start? Sometimes a husband will say or do something foolish, and everything in you wants to correct him on the spot in front of others, especially if you think you're helping him. But here's the trick: when you choose not to humiliate him, you're sending a powerful message. You're saying, *"You are more important to me than the mistakes you make, and I'm not going to harm our relationship by putting you down."* That's the essence of respect and grace in marriage.

Scripture says, *"A gentle answer turns away wrath, but a harsh word stirs up anger"* (Proverbs 15:1). Public correction almost always feels like a harsh word to a man—it stirs up defensiveness, not connection. Grace, on the other hand, makes space for growth.

Respect isn't about pretending your husband is flawless. It's about choosing to build him up instead of tearing him down. It's about speaking highly of him, even in front of others—sometimes even prophesying the man he *will become,* not just commenting on who he *is today.* That kind of faith in him can set the course for his divine destiny.

Dave says he is where he is today, in large part, because I chose to believe in him when no one else did. That doesn't mean I've never seen his weaknesses—it means I've learned that my role is to be his greatest encourager, not his sharpest critic. When I treat him with respect, I'm not ignoring his flaws; I'm creating an environment where he can grow beyond them. He does the same for me and encourages me regularly. We've grown into a strong team, and we both understand that together we are stronger than we ever could be separately.

Paul writes in Colossians 3:8–10 that we're to put off old habits—anger, malice, harsh speech—and put on the new self, renewed in the image of our Creator. In marriage, this means actively replacing old habits—such as criticism, disrespect, dishonesty, neglect, and defensiveness—with new actions like encouragement, affection, kindness, and attentive listening.

One of the simplest ways to change the climate of a marriage is to replace one old habit with a new and positive action every week. If you've been quick to criticize, start each day with a word of affirmation instead. If neglect has crept in, make a point to connect daily, even if it's just for a few minutes. These small changes add up—and over time, they can completely transform the emotional tone of your relationship.

> **Practical Takeaway:** Replace one negative habit with a positive action every week for a month—even if your spouse is not ready to join you in making changes. Watch how the small, intentional choices to respect, focus, affirm, and encourage your partner can create a marriage where joy grows naturally.

CHAPTER TWELVE

Being Heard

| *Denise's perspective* |

I WAS ENROLLED IN A year-long personal coaching course when Dave and I first met. Part of the program involved group calls during which we practiced new ways to communicate. Dave was invited to listen in, and I don't think either of us realized at the time how much those simple exercises would reshape the way in which we communicate.

One of the exercises was harder than it sounded: listening to another person for as long as they needed to talk—without interrupting, judging, or offering a quick solution. The rule was simple: no responses, no corrections, no advice. Just be present and listen. For many of us, this exercise was awkward at first. But then something powerful happened. People who had carried wounds for years found themselves breaking down in tears—not because they were offered answers, but because they were finally given the freedom to speak. They felt safe. They felt heard.

For me, that was life-changing. I realized how rare it was to speak without being cut off, or to be honest without fear of criticism. In past relationships, I often felt like my words had to fight for air, as if the other person was only half-listening while already preparing their response. But during those coaching exercises, I discovered something different. I felt what it was like to share my heart and have someone listen all the way through. And I knew—I needed this in marriage.

The Bible says it beautifully in James 1:19: *"Everyone should be quick to listen, slow to speak and slow to become angry."* That verse became real to me in those moments. Listening first changes everything. It tells the person speaking: *You matter. Your voice matters. Your heart is safe with me.*

I've come to realize that there's a significant difference between reacting and responding. A *reaction* is typically quick, often defensive, and sometimes sharp. It stems from raw emotion—anger, fear, and pride—and can wound more deeply than we realize. A *response*, on the other hand, is slower. It comes after you've listened, after you've let the words land, after you've asked God how to answer with gentleness—reactions close doors. Responses open them.

We first learned to practice this with other students in the coaching class and then applied it in everyday conversations with friends and family members. At first, I got confused looks from my teenage son sitting across the table from me in the morning. He didn't understand why I wasn't jumping in with a quick reaction to whatever he was telling me. I explained that I was learning how to listen and respond, rather than immediately react.

When Dave and I began practicing this with each other, it was revolutionary. Imagine being able to share something heavy or vulnerable and not receiving defensiveness, criticism, or an instant fix-it answer—just listening and caring.

For me, it was healing. It built trust. It proved I wasn't alone. Most of the time, I didn't need advice anyway. I just needed to know he heard me. Proverbs 18:13 says, *"To answer before listening—that is folly and shame."* That scripture captures so many of my past experiences. But when Dave chose to hold back and listen, he gave me a gift words alone could never provide.

Really listening takes effort—and practice. It means putting down your phone, focusing, making eye contact, and allowing someone to express themselves fully (even if it's criticism). It means biting your tongue when you want to lash out and defend yourself. It means reminding yourself: *I am listening now, just listening. I'm holding my emotions in check. No interrupting.*

Then, when it's your turn to talk, you might ask questions if you need clarification to understand something they're saying. If your emotions are too high to give a careful response, ask for time to process your thoughts. Make a plan to speak with them again later that day, or on another day. There is nothing wrong with delaying your response. In fact, seeking wisdom first in an emotional situation will help you avoid a reactionary reply that you'll regret later.

When Dave chooses to *respond* instead of *react*, the atmosphere of our marriage changes. I feel valued. He feels connected. And together, we walk away with peace instead of tension. That's the gift of listening—it builds bridges where arguments would have built walls.

CHAPTER THIRTEEN

Boundaries in Marriage

| *Dave's perspective* |

FOR MOST OF MY LIFE, I struggled with codependency. I didn't call it that at the time—I just thought I was "being helpful" or "keeping the peace." But in reality, my relationships were a constant tug-of-war, full of subtle manipulation, unspoken expectations, and the low-grade anxiety that comes from trying to make everyone else happy. I was in my fifties before I understood that I could not please everyone.

Codependency sometimes masquerades as a caring attitude, but it's really control in disguise. I thought I was managing situations for the good of the relationship, but what I was actually doing was wearing myself out and robbing the relationship of genuine joy. My sense of self-worth was tied to keeping the other person satisfied, which meant I often ignored my own needs and overstepped my own limits. That kind of dynamic isn't just exhausting—it's unhealthy for both people involved.

In their book *Boundaries: When to Say Yes and How to Say No,* Dr. Henry Cloud and Dr. John Townsend define boundaries as invisible 'property lines' that define our responsibilities and protect our values and well-being. Denise introduced me to this book because its bible-based principles were so helpful in her life.

Everything began to change when I learned about healthy boundaries. At first, the idea seemed foreign. I thought boundaries were about building walls and keeping people out. But I came to understand that boundaries are more like fences with gates—you get to decide what comes in and what goes out. They define where you end and the other person begins.

Setting boundaries was not easy for me. When you've spent years saying 'yes' to everything, suddenly saying 'no' feels like a crime. And when you finally do start setting boundaries, people push back—especially if they've grown used to you accommodating them. In marriage, that pushback can be uncomfortable. It can even trigger conflict. But here's the surprising thing I've learned: conflict isn't always a bad sign. In fact, when you're setting healthy boundaries, conflict can be a sign that you're on the right track.

Jesus modeled boundaries in His ministry. He walked away from crowds when it was time to rest. He didn't let people dictate His schedule. He chose when to engage and when to withdraw, all while living in perfect love. When you set and enforce healthy boundaries, you're not withholding love—you're loving wisely.

In our marriage, boundaries have been a game-changer. They've helped me protect my mental and emotional health, and they've freed Denise from the invisible strings of manipulation that come with codependency. Boundaries keep me honest about what I can and can't do, what I will and won't accept. They create space for both of us to be fully ourselves without stepping on each other's identities or responsibilities.

If you're new to boundaries, expect the early stages to be awkward. You might feel guilty for protecting your own time, energy, or emotional well-being. You might face resistance from your spouse or others in your life. But remember this: a healthy marriage isn't one where you give until there's nothing left—it's one where both people are free to give joyfully, from a place of wholeness.

When you hit that first round of pushback, don't panic. Rejoice. It means you're changing the old patterns. You're breaking free from cycles that have drained you and laying the groundwork for a marriage built on mutual respect instead of silent resentment.

Boundaries aren't the enemy of love—they're the framework that allows love to grow strong without getting tangled in control, fear, or manipulation. And once you start living with them, you'll wonder how you ever managed without them.

How to Start Building Healthy Boundaries Together

If you and your spouse want to make boundaries a healthy, normal part of your relationship, here's how to begin:

Have an honest conversation about needs. Take turns sharing the emotional, physical, and spiritual needs that matter most to each of you. You can't protect what you haven't identified.

Agree on what's non-negotiable. These are the areas where boundaries are essential—such as fidelity, honesty, respect, and time alone with God.

Use "I" statements. Boundaries work best when they are framed in terms of your own limits, not demands on the other person. For example: "I need time to rest after work before I'm ready to talk about heavy topics."

Keep communication open. Boundaries are not set in stone. Life changes, seasons shift, and you may need to adjust them. Revisit your agreements regularly.

Support each other's boundaries. This is where trust grows. Respecting your spouse's boundaries—even when they're inconvenient—shows you value them as a person, not just a role.

Boundaries, when practiced together, create the safety and trust that make intimacy possible. They allow both husband and wife to bring their whole selves to the marriage—not out of fear, but out of freedom.

CHAPTER FOURTEEN

Financial Unity

| *Dave's perspective* |

MARRIAGE WITHOUT FINANCIAL UNITY IS like a boat with two captains trying to steer in opposite directions—you're going to end up somewhere you never intended to go, and it probably won't be a good place.

A lack of financial unity was one of the key factors that led to the end of my first marriage. I had always carried the conviction that I should be the sole provider for my family. I worked hard and made sure the bills could be paid. My priority was to keep us financially secure—paying for housing, keeping the lights on, and ensuring our basic needs were met before anything clsc.

But my ex-wife didn't see things that way. Her approach to money was more about immediate needs—or sometimes wants—than about long-term stability. When our spending outpaced our income, she didn't see it as a major problem. I did. That difference in priorities caused friction.

It started with arguments over small purchases. Then, little by little, the strain grew heavier. Bills went unpaid. First came bankruptcy. Then, the truck payment fell behind. Eventually, we lost our home. It wasn't just the financial loss that hurt—it was the deep sense of instability and the erosion of trust. Looking back, the damage to our marriage had already begun long before the bank sent a foreclosure notice.

When Denise and I met, I knew one of the first serious conversations we needed to have was about money. We both had some battle scars when it came to finances, and I didn't want to repeat old mistakes. Early on, we laid all our cards on the table—how we viewed money, our priorities, our past mistakes, and our long-term hopes.

We agreed on something simple but vital: in our marriage, financial decisions would be made together. That means we both know where the money is going, and neither of us is making big financial commitments without the other's knowledge or agreement. We decided bills would be paid first. That was non-negotiable. We would live within our means, even if that meant saying no to something we wanted in the moment.

Have we had times when money was tight? Absolutely. But because we've disciplined ourselves to stay united, those seasons didn't become sources of division. Instead, they became opportunities to lean on God together. More than once, we've seen His provision in ways we couldn't have orchestrated ourselves—unexpected income, a reduced bill, a timely monetary gift from someone who had no idea we were in need. We've learned that unity in finances isn't just about numbers—it's about faith, trust, and shared stewardship.

The Bible says we are not owners, but stewards. Everything we have belongs to God, and He entrusts us with resources to manage for His purposes. Financial unity is aligning our household with Kingdom priorities. When a couple walks in agreement in this area, money becomes a tool for building, blessing, and investing in what matters most, instead of a weapon that wounds the relationship.

If you and your spouse are struggling with financial unity, start by having the conversations you've been avoiding. Lay everything out on the table—debts, accounts, spending habits, fears, and hopes. If this seems too difficult, consider searching for a class or a coach who can help you move past your fears and take steps to make a change.

Pray together over your finances. Invite God into the center of your financial decisions. When you agree with each other and with Him, you'll find that peace in your marriage doesn't depend on the size of your bank account, but on the strength of your partnership and the faithfulness of your God.

CHAPTER FIFTEEN

Parenting as One

| *Denise's perspective* |

WHEN DAVE AND I MARRIED, we didn't just blend our lives—we blended our families. He had two children, and I had a son. If you've ever been part of a blended family, you know this is more than just a logistical challenge—it's an emotional one.

I had been listening to a Christian counseling radio program for several years. Callers to the show would ask for help with their family issues. Practical steps, grounded in biblical principles, formed the basis for the advice callers received from the hosts. Listening to the struggles of others taught me that I would have to seek wisdom when stepping into my new role as a stepparent. I looked for books to help guide me. After searching for articles and books, I found very little. The small bit of advice I was able to discover addressed the issue of who should discipline the children in a blended family if problems arose with the kids.

From the outset, we realized that our parenting styles would require careful coordination. There's an unspoken loyalty in children toward their biological parent that can make them resistant to guidance from a stepparent. My 19-year-old son would likely struggle to receive instruction from Dave. His 14-year-old twins might resent me if I had to correct or discipline them. All of us would be adjusting to our new family life; some choppy waters should be expected.

Given the advice that children generally respond better when the biological parent enforces the rules, we decided to follow that as much as possible. We agreed that it would prevent tension not only with the kids but also between us as a couple. Of course, we both wanted to be respected by all of our kids, but we came to understand that building influence takes time, and forcing it usually does more harm than good. By honoring the natural bond between parent and child, we laid a foundation of trust that eventually made room for guidance from the stepparent as well.

Why Unity Matters

The bigger issue here isn't just discipline—it's unity. When parents aren't united, kids sense it immediately. They pick up on the tiniest cracks in the foundation and sometimes use them to their advantage. This is true in any household, but in a blended family, the potential for division can be even greater.

Unity in parenting didn't mean we always agreed in the moment; instead, we discussed disagreements privately and presented a united front to the children. If one of us had a stance but the other disagreed, we would discuss it later, out of earshot of the kids. This strategy protected our relationship, modeled respect, and avoided undermining each other's authority. It also kept us from sending mixed messages to the kids.

The Bible reminds us in Amos 3:3, *"Do two walk together unless they have agreed to do so?"* Agreement doesn't mean uniformity, but it does mean alignment. Walking together as one is a choice that couples can make daily, even when emotions run high.

Spirit-Led Parenting

Being united also means being Spirit-led in our parenting. We've both had moments where the Holy Spirit prompted us to go in a different direction than we had planned—whether it was showing extra grace in a moment of failure, or being firm when compromise would have been easier. Spirit-led parenting requires prayer, humility, and the willingness to listen to God before reacting.

Sometimes that meant pausing before speaking, asking for wisdom in the midst of an argument, or admitting when we hadn't handled something well. Our kids saw not just our decisions, but also our dependence on God in the process. That might have been as much a lesson to them as any rule we enforced.

Protecting the Marriage First

I'm grateful for the wisdom we gained during those early years. They weren't easy lessons. At times, it felt like the kids weren't happy with the situation. We all struggled to navigate the challenges, but we learned to protect the unity of our marriage—even when making parenting decisions was difficult.

It's tempting to let children drive the household, especially when you want to keep the peace. But kids feel more secure when they know their parents remain stable in the midst of difficult times.

The Legacy We Leave

Our goal wasn't to win every conflict with our kids, but to create a home where love, respect, and God's presence guide our decisions. We didn't do it perfectly, but we learned that if we stood together as one, our children would not just understand the rules—they would see how we worked with each other through some difficult times.

Now, our kids have begun to parent their own children. They'll most likely face the same challenges of unity, discipline, and balance. What will matter most is not whether we enforced every house rule or got every decision right, but whether we tried our best to honor God, respect each other, and create an atmosphere of stability for the family.

CHAPTER SIXTEEN

The Enemy at the Gate

| *Dave's Perspective* |

JESUS DIDN'T MINCE WORDS ABOUT the nature of our spiritual adversary. He told us plainly in John 10:10, *"The thief comes only to steal and kill and destroy; I have come that they may have life, and have it to the full."* The devil's tactics may be ancient, but they're as aggressive and personal today as they were in the first century. If he can't pull you away from God, he'll try to drive a wedge between you and your spouse.

Denise and I have lived this truth. My work as a writer has often taken me into controversial territory. I've written about subjects that powerful people wanted to remain buried. For a time, I enjoyed success—my books sold well, and our online community grew quickly. But one day, the hammer came down. My bestselling titles were blacklisted. My social media accounts were suspended. Payment processors shut down our accounts without warning. Overnight, our income and our ability to reach people were in jeopardy. It was clear to both of us that this wasn't just business opposition—it was spiritual warfare. I had kicked the hornet's nest, and the powers that be retaliated. The goal was to isolate us, silence us, and strip us of the resources we needed to keep going.

How the Enemy Attacks Marriage

When the enemy comes against your calling and your ability to pay the bills, he's almost always aiming at your connection as a couple. Why? Because if he can divide you, he's already won half the battle. Division breeds discouragement, and discouragement chokes faith. Suddenly, minor irritations can become major arguments, trust feels shaky, and unity is replaced by suspicion or blame. Stress has a way of making molehills look like mountains inside a marriage.

For Denise and me, the temptation was real. I felt pressure as the provider. She felt the weight of uncertainty about the future. If we weren't careful, we could have ended up pointing fingers instead of holding hands. That's exactly what the enemy wanted.

Our Deliberate Choice

That's why, from the beginning of that battle, we made a conscious choice to face this together, united in Christ. We reminded ourselves that we weren't each other's enemies. The devil was the enemy, and he had just made the mistake of showing his hand.

We prayed together daily—not just quick prayers, but focused, specific petitions for God's wisdom, protection, and provision. We asked Him to expose the enemy's schemes and give us His strategy for moving forward. Sometimes that meant praying over our finances. At other times, it meant praying for our attitudes toward each other so that we wouldn't let stress get the upper hand.

In time, the Holy Spirit revealed a plan. It was a step-by-step roadmap for how to weather the storm, adjust our methods, and come out on the other side without losing what mattered most.

Locking Shields

God's guidance in that season didn't just preserve our livelihood—it strengthened our marriage. We learned the power of locking shields, of refusing to give in to fear, and of holding fast to God's promises even when the circumstances looked grim.

The image of Roman soldiers locking shields in formation comes to mind. Alone, each shield only covered part of the soldier. But side by side, their shields created a nearly impenetrable wall. That's what prayer and unity did for us. Where I was weak, Denise was strong. Where she was discouraged, I could encourage her. Together, we became a wall the enemy couldn't easily penetrate.

First Peter 5:8–9 warns us to *"be alert and of sober mind"* because the enemy prowls around like a roaring lion. But the very next verse tells us to *"resist him, standing firm in the faith."* Standing firm isn't a solo activity—it's something you do together, shoulder to shoulder, as one.

Your Marriage Is Worth Defending

If you've noticed a repeated pattern of conflict or pressure in your marriage—something that seems to flare up at key moments or target your unity—it might not be random. It could be an intentional strike from the enemy. Don't take the bait. Don't let him turn you against each other. Instead, bring it into the light. Name it for what it is. Pray together over it. Speak God's Word into it. Ask the Lord for His strategy, because He always has one. And remember—your marriage is worth defending. It's not just about you, but about the testimony of what God can do when two people stand united under His banner.

When the enemy comes to the gate of your marriage, don't panic. Stand together and remember that the One who called you is faithful. He will never abandon you.

CHAPTER SEVENTEEN

Praying with Your Spouse

| *Denise's Perspective* |

EVEN THOUGH DAVE IS A former atheist, he's not bad when it comes to prayer. In fact, one of the pleasant surprises in our marriage has been discovering how naturally he steps into that role. Before we met and married, I had made a quiet decision in my heart: I wanted my husband to be the spiritual leader in our home. I didn't know who he would be yet, but I knew I wanted a man who would pray over our family. Thankfully, Dave has been happy to assume that responsibility.

Not every woman is so fortunate. Many men shy away from the idea of being the spiritual leader in their marriage. Some feel unqualified. Others are intimidated. Still others just never had a model for what that looked like. But, leadership in prayer doesn't require perfection—it just requires a willing heart. A husband doesn't need eloquent words to pray with his wife; he only needs sincerity and the courage to begin.

Overcoming the Barriers

In many marriages, prayer feels awkward at first. Couples who can talk for hours about their day sometimes freeze when it's time to pray together. Why? Because prayer reveals what's in our hearts. It exposes vulnerability. And vulnerability, even in marriage, can feel risky. But prayer was never meant to be polished or intimidating—it's a conversation with God, together.

If praying out loud feels daunting, start with small steps. One of you can thank God for something good that happened that day. The other can pray for strength for tomorrow. Don't focus on length or depth at first. Focus on consistency. Over time, that consistency will breed comfort, and comfort will open the door to deeper prayers.

Learning to Flow Together

Years ago, God gave me a glimpse of the power of praying in tongues when my neighbor prayed over me in difficult times. I didn't understand the spiritual language, but I was drawn to the beauty of it and the flow. After I married Dave, we attended a church where people would speak and even sing in tongues during worship. It was still a bit mysterious and foreign to me, but the more I saw it, the more I wanted to experience that deeper dimension of prayer. At one point, I was prompted in my own private prayer time to try, and before long, praying in tongues became the most natural way for me to pray.

Today, when Dave and I pray together, we have a rhythm that works for us. He leads, and I follow. He prays in English as the Holy Spirit leads him—sometimes for our life, or our kids, and sometimes for others who are in need. As he prays, I pray in tongues. It's not a formula or a magic trick. It's just the way we've found to flow together in prayer. The words may be different, but the Spirit is the same.

That flow didn't come overnight; it grew over time. Now it feels as natural as breathing. And that's the point: prayer with your spouse doesn't have to be perfect—it just has to be practiced. You'll soon discover what feels comfortable for you as a couple.

The Power of Agreement

There is a unique authority in united prayer. Jesus said in Matthew 18:19, *"If two of you agree on earth about anything they ask, it will be done for them by my Father in heaven."* That promise is for every believing couple. When you pray in agreement, you're not just strengthening your marriage—you're pushing back against the enemy's schemes and advancing God's purposes together.

We've seen this firsthand. There have been seasons when finances were tight, work was uncertain, or family issues weighed heavily on our hearts. The turning point wasn't just us coming up with a solution—it was us agreeing in prayer, and asking God to move. Over and over, we've seen Him answer in ways we couldn't have orchestrated.

Prayer not only changes circumstances—it changes us. It softens hard hearts. It brings hidden fears into the open. It turns arguments into moments of humility.

Building a Fortress Around Your Marriage

The enemy wants silence between spouses. Silence breeds distance. But prayer fosters intimacy, both with God and with one another. It's one of the most powerful ways to fortify your marriage against attack. When you and your spouse pray together, you're doing more than talking to God—you're building a fortress around your covenant.

If discomfort is holding you back. Start simple. Take turns praying short prayers over each other. Read a psalm together and turn it into a prayer. Ask God for the courage to lead, or the humility to follow.

Prayer isn't about performance—it's about connection. It's about inviting God into your life together and agreeing for His will to be done. And when you do that, you'll discover that prayer isn't just something you add to marriage—it's something that holds it together.

CHAPTER EIGHTEEN

Hearing God Together

| *Dave's Perspective* |

AT TIMES, LEARNING TO HEAR God together can feel like navigating a minefield. There are so many variables—our personal desires, our blind spots, our emotions—that can color what we believe we're hearing from Him. But when you set aside personal agendas and seek wisdom, the process can become one of the most spiritually enriching times in your marriage.

Shortly after Denise and I married, I began having vivid dreams, visions, and personal encounters with God. Some were deeply symbolic; others were startlingly clear. Denise also had dreams and spiritual encounters that held messages. It's tempting, when you're the one receiving a message, to assume you now hold the "final word" on what God is saying. But that mindset is dangerous in a marriage. Wisdom dictates that revelation from God must be evaluated together, with both spouses having a voice in discerning the true meaning.

When God speaks, we both listen. Sometimes that listening is quiet and prayerful. Sometimes it means taking a few days to reflect. And then—because we're both coffee people—we pour a couple of mugs and sit down at the table. We talk through what we saw or heard, or the symbolism we sensed in the message. We ask each other questions: *Does this align with God's word and character? Does it confirm something He's already spoken to us? Should we act or wait for more?*

Many times, the precise meaning of a confusing dream has popped into my head—not while I was trying to decode it alone, but in the middle of our discussion. And just as often, the "aha" moment has come through Denise's insight. I've learned that God often plants pieces of the puzzle in both of us, so that we're forced to come together to see the full picture. It's His way of keeping us united in the process.

Hearing God together also protects us from one of the oldest tricks in the book: using "God told me" as a trump card to get our way. That seems like manipulation dressed in spiritual language—not discernment. When one spouse pulls the "God told me" card without inviting the other into the discernment process, it creates imbalance, resentment, and mistrust. But when both spouses work together to discern the message, it gains credibility and shared ownership.

God loves to speak to couples because He loves unity. When we humble ourselves, set aside personal preferences, and give Him the final say, we not only hear more clearly—we also find ourselves walking in greater confidence and peace. And as a bonus, we get to watch our spiritual intimacy deepen right alongside our marital bond.

Three Filters for Discerning God's Voice as a Couple

1. The Scripture Filter – If what you've heard or seen runs against the principles, commands, or spirit of the Bible, it's not from Him. This filter is the first and most important test—if it doesn't pass here, it stops here.

2. The Character Filter – Ask: *Does this sound like the God we know?* God's voice will reflect His nature—love, mercy, holiness, patience, truth. If the message stirs fear, condemnation, or manipulation without the hope of redemption, it's worth pressing pause and seeking clarity.

3. The Peace Filter – Even when God's direction is challenging, it will be accompanied by a deep inner peace that transcends circumstances. If one spouse feels unsettled, it's a sign to slow down, pray more, and wait for confirmation. Unity in peace is better than haste in uncertainty.

Below, I want to share a story I wrote that was previously published in *My Craziest Adventures with God - Volume 1*. This is an abbreviated version. It illustrates how a promise from God inspired us to push through a difficult situation.

When Wells Fargo Tells You to Pray

Moving from Washington State to Arizona was a big step. Our move wasn't something God actually told us to do. From the beginning, we realized it was completely our decision to move. The weather, lower housing prices, and several other factors made it a desirable location for us.

Prior to moving, amidst all our planning, I didn't have a single dream about Arizona, except for one dream that occurred three weeks before our move. One morning, I woke up from a dream and, as usual,

I wrote it down on an index card so I wouldn't forget it. A few minutes later, Denise woke up. I said to her, "I had an interesting dream, honey."

"So did I," she replied."

I gave her a kiss. "Why don't you tell me yours first?"

She said, "I was in an office—I think, at a title company—sitting at a desk signing papers to close on a home loan."

I looked at her and began giggling. "You're not going to believe this. I had the same dream!"

"What do you mean the same dream?"

"In my dream, I was in an office signing documents to close on a home loan."

"Are you serious?" She asked.

"Dead serious. You know... I've always wanted us to have the same dream on the same night. Never thought it would happen."

When we moved, we decided to do a short-term (month-to-month) lease on an apartment in Mesa, Arizona. We didn't want to commit to a one-year lease on a small apartment, as we believed we would find a home to buy quickly. Sure enough, within two weeks of moving, we found the house we wanted. We made an offer, and it was accepted. We began making plans and started collecting documents for the home loan.

To qualify for the loan, we had some problems to overcome. I took a 50% cut in pay when I relocated to Arizona, and Denise hadn't found a job yet. We had to qualify based on my income alone, and that meant I had to work a lot of overtime to demonstrate to the bank that we could afford the loan. We had another problem concerning my hourly pay. My employer agreed to an hourly wage increase if I could prove I'd never had a lapse in my paramedic license, going all the way back to 1988. It took several weeks and numerous phone calls, but I gathered what they wanted. After all that, my employer decided not to honor the agreement. They started me at the bottom of the pay scale, and the raise they ultimately decided to give was less than what we agreed to—and didn't come in a timely manner.

The week before the bank was going to look at my paycheck to see if I would qualify for the loan, I still had not received the raise my employer had promised. We knew if the company didn't change my wage immediately, we wouldn't qualify. So, after I got off duty that Friday, I called the human resources department at work. Unfortunately, it was 4:30 p.m. and the office was about to close for the weekend. Nothing like last-minute details! I had 30 minutes to get through to find out what was going on with my raise. I kept having problems getting through to a real person and even got disconnected a few times, sending Denise into near panic. I was finally transferred to a real person, but it wasn't the right person. Time was running short. This craziness went on until one employee finally sensed our urgency, left her desk, and walked through the building looking for someone who could help me.

The answer was not what we wanted; the general manager had not approved my raise because he was in the hospital. The company's payroll would be distributed on Monday morning. The change had to be approved by then, or our window of opportunity would be gone. We prayed. Actually, we had been praying a lot even prior to this because we went through almost daily setbacks in this loan process. My prayer was basically a declaration. In my heart, I felt the dream God gave us was a promise that we'd get the house. A few of our friends were in on the drama, and they prayed with us.

I knew there was no one in the company working over the weekend who could approve my raise. Realistically, it couldn't happen. But on Monday morning, I still needed to see if God had worked some sort of miracle over the weekend. I logged on to the company website out of curiosity to check on my hourly pay rate. Much to my surprise, my raise went through over the weekend! I was so surprised that I drove to the human resources office to talk to someone about it. I met with the same woman who took my phone call on Friday afternoon.

"Hi, I spoke with you on Friday about my raise. I logged on to the company website this morning out of curiosity to see if my raise went through. I was really surprised to see that it was approved. I almost can't believe it's true. Would you check on it in your records?"

"Really? That's odd. I was under the impression it wouldn't be approved since the division general manager has to approve it and he's been in the hospital. Let me take a look." She logged onto the website and checked. "Well it seems you're right. Your raise was approved sometime Friday afternoon."

"I don't mean to sound ungrateful. I'm happy the raise was approved, but if the general manager was in the hospital and he couldn't approve my raise, who did?"

"I have no idea."

"Thank you. I guess we'll be going now." I began to wonder if maybe God sent an angel into the manager's office to approve my raise. Yay God! But we're not out of the woods yet.

The home inspection was done, and some minor repairs to the roof and the gate were needed. The inspector was certain the loan would not go through until the repairs had been made. We expected to hear from the owner about how we'd get the repairs done before closing, but the call never came.

Then, we got a call from our loan officer, who informed us that underwriting was requiring no repairs to the home before closing. We were shocked. So was the loan officer. "I've been doing loans a long time, and this is the first time I've ever seen this happen. They always find something that needs to be fixed. I don't get it." So he double-checked with underwriting, and sure enough—we could close without making any repairs. This is how the entire process went—one potential obstacle after another, followed by an unexpected and hard-to-believe solution that miraculously materialized.

Then, more problems cropped up in underwriting. My income, which included a lot of overtime, was in question. They contacted my employer several times to verify the facts, and every time they did, my employer provided information that made things even worse.

One Friday afternoon, our loan officer called Denise with more bad news. "Hi guys. How are you doing? It's been a pretty hectic week with underwriting. I was wondering if you guys believe in prayer."

Denise replied, "We've been praying ever since we made the offer. What's going on?"

"You'll probably want to keep praying this weekend. You're going to need some help if the loan is going to go through. We don't have a clear-cut answer from underwriting yet. It looks like you've got a borderline case—it could go either way. It's completely up to the discretion of the underwriter."

I'll admit we were concerned. But every time worry reared its head, we thought about the dreams and about all the things God had already done for us.

It seemed that every Friday, the loan officer would call with bad news. We'd pray and make declarations over the weekend. On Monday or Tuesday, he would call with good news. That's how it went week after week.

Despite the uncertainties, we gave notice to our landlord that we were moving out of the apartment and scheduled movers—although we still had no firm approval or closing date for the home loan.

One day, Denise received another call from the bank. "Guys, we're coming down to the wire regarding your earnest money. The time is fast approaching when you will lose your earnest money if the loan doesn't go through. You have to make a choice. You either keep your offer on the table and hope you're approved (at the risk of losing your money) or you can withdraw your offer and the funds will be returned to you."

The stress of this decision was immense, but after the roller-coaster process we had been through, we knew we had to hold onto our dream from God. Denise explained to our loan officer, "We both had a dream on the same night that we were in an office signing papers to close on the loan. We're taking it as a promise from God that the loan will be approved, so we're keeping our offer on the table."

It was a good decision as we were eventually approved for the loan.

Various other obstacles and delays arose even after approval—the full details are in my previous book. So, I'll fast forward to the actual closing day. Our movers started early, picking up boxes and furniture at our apartment. Denise and I were asked to be at the title company to sign documents in a town about 30 minutes away. After the signing, it was odd that no one gave us keys to the house. Our movers started unloading our furniture into the driveway of our new home because they couldn't get in. Calls were made, and our Realtor finally asked us to check inside the breaker panel outside the house. We looked, and sure enough, we found a key hidden inside.

The process of moving and buying the house was one of the most stressful and yet one of the most splendidly divine ordeals I've ever been through. The hand of God was all over this thing. And the crowning jewel came about a week later when we received a call from our loan officer. "I want to congratulate you two on pulling off one of the craziest home purchases I've ever witnessed. I also want to apologize for how the closing was delayed. We really dropped the ball on this one. I feel terrible about all the trouble we put you through. The bank wants to show its appreciation for your business, so they've authorized me to make a donation on behalf of the bank, in the amount equal to one month's mortgage to the charity of your choice in your name so you'll receive the tax deduction for the donation. So, we'll need some information about the charity you'd like to choose."

We were speechless. Who ever heard of a mortgage company donating to a charity because they made a mistake? We gave him the name of a ministry run by a friend in another state. It was operating on a shoestring budget. I called the guy in charge of the ministry and gave him the news. "Now I need some information from you so the bank can make the donation." He was elated by the news, but he had some news of his own to share.

"You're not going to believe this," he said.

"Try me."

"Yesterday I was praying, and for some reason I asked God to send someone from Arizona to help finance something He had put on my heart. I wasn't even sure I knew anyone in Arizona. Today you called with the answer to my prayer."

The ministry received the donation from Wells Fargo Bank, and we had a nice tax deduction that year, courtesy of the Chief Financial Officer of heaven. In the midst of our loan process, we would have preferred smooth sailing rather than all the turmoil. But looking back, we're grateful God had the bigger picture.

Although you may have never had the same nighttime dream as your spouse, you may hear God together in other ways—through Holy Spirit prompts, or thought impressions when you need to make a decision together. When we choose to listen together, we gain a shared confidence that God will guide, protect, and provide—even when the road feels rough. And sometimes, what He shows us isn't just encouragement but an invitation to clear out anything that could hinder His work in our lives. That's where the next chapter takes us—into the powerful, practical work of deliverance, where we learn to shut the enemy out and keep our marriage a place where God's presence can freely lead us forward.

CHAPTER NINETEEN

Deliverance for Couples

| *Dave's Perspective* |

IN THE LAST CHAPTER, WE discussed hearing God together—listening for His voice and discerning His direction as a couple. Sometimes, what we hear from Him leads us to deeper intimacy and joy. At other times, it may expose something far darker—hidden footholds that the enemy has been using to undermine us. That's where deliverance comes in.

Being a former atheist, I'll be honest—the whole subject of deliverance used to sound corny to me. I pictured strange church services with shouting, flailing, and people rolling around on the floor. Even after I'd been a believer for years, I saw no need for it. In my mind, Christians didn't have demons—end of discussion. But then one day, God opened my eyes to the reality of the spiritual world. It began with the simple instruction I heard Him whisper: *Pray for your patients.* I was a paramedic at the time. So, awkwardly, hesitantly, I started offering prayer. At first, nothing happened. But over time, I began witnessing miracles—real healings that had no medical explanation. People's bodies changed. Pain disappeared. Hearts and minds were restored. And that's when the demons came knocking.

New Levels, New Devils

There's a saying in ministry: *New levels, new devils.* When you step into new territory in the Kingdom, you also step onto the enemy's radar. The resistance changes. The opposition gets smarter. For me, the shift was evident. It wasn't just random hardship anymore—it was targeted. Accusations out of nowhere. Strife over small things. Sleep disruption. Unexplained aches and pains. It didn't take long to realize: some of these battles weren't natural at all. Paul warned us in Ephesians 6:12 that *"our struggle is not against flesh and blood, but against rulers, authorities, powers of this dark world, and spiritual forces of evil in the heavenly realms."* Once you accept that truth, you stop wasting energy fighting the wrong battles. The enemy's goal is simple: divide you from God, divide you from your spouse, and derail the assignment God has placed on your life.

Why Couples Must Face This Together

Denise and I had to learn quickly how to handle this as a team. Deliverance isn't just for "someone else out there." It's a spiritual tool every believer—and especially every married couple—should have in their arsenal. Here's why: when two become one flesh, the enemy doesn't just attack individuals—he attacks the covenant. If one spouse is bound, weighed down, or deceived, the ripple effects hit both. That's why unity in deliverance is so important.

Closing Doors

We began praying not just for God's blessing, but for the breaking of every assignment against our marriage, our home, and our calling. We learned to close spiritual doors where the enemy might gain an entryway to divide and disrupt.

Handling issues like unforgiveness, bitterness, hidden sin, or even careless words spoken is more important than some realize. These aren't harmless quirks; they're invitations to the enemy. And when one spouse opens that door, the whole marriage is vulnerable. For example:

Unforgiveness gives Satan leverage (Ephesians 4:26–27).

Hidden sin breeds shame, which isolates instead of unites.

Negative declarations ("You'll never change" or "This marriage won't last") act like curses spoken into the atmosphere.

The good news? Every open door that allows access to demons can be closed by the blood of Jesus.

Deliverance Is About Authority

Deliverance, at its core, is not about theatrics—it's about authority. Jesus said in Luke 10:19, *"I have given you authority to trample on snakes and scorpions and to overcome all the power of the enemy; nothing will harm you."* That authority doesn't come from shouting louder—it comes from knowing who you are in Christ and standing in agreement with His Word.

Deliverance can become part of your spiritual rhythm together: you pray, you listen for direction, and when necessary, you evict intruders. Sometimes that looks like breaking an agreement with lies you've believed. Sometimes it means renouncing generational patterns that have been repeated in your family. At other times, it's commanding spirits of pain and sickness to leave and never return.

A Marriage Secured

Over time, Denise and I have come to realize that practicing deliverance together doesn't just keep us free—it keeps us close. It builds trust. Deliverance isn't just about casting out darkness—it's about making more room for God's light. And when a couple commits to that process together, they discover a marriage that is lighter, freer, and more resilient than they ever thought possible.

CHAPTER TWENTY

Emotional Healing

| *Dave's Perspective* |

WHEN MOST PEOPLE HEAR THE word *deliverance*, they picture a messy scene—someone screaming, thrashing on the floor, maybe a loud voice commanding a demon to leave. I've seen that version. It happens, but deliverance doesn't have to be dramatic to be effective.

Years ago, God took me on a very different journey. It began when He started showing me my own broken places—past wounds I'd ignored, papered over, or tried to muscle through. I didn't know it at the time, but those old hurts had left open doors in my life—what Paul calls "footholds" in Ephesians 4:26–27. They were access points for the enemy. That's when I started studying emotional healing. I didn't just skim the surface; I dove deep. I went through more than a dozen different methods—everything from inner healing prayer models to counseling-based techniques. Each had its strengths, but I found myself asking God for something simpler. Something anyone could do.

And then the Holy Spirit showed me a process that changed everything. It was quick. It was gentle. It got to the root without digging people into a deeper hole. And here's the most surprising part—when you heal the wound, the demon often leaves on its own: no shouting, no theatrics, no exorcist soundtrack playing in the background.

Demons feed on pain, bitterness, and lies we've believed about ourselves. Take away the pain, replace the lie with truth, and the spirit loses its legal right to stay. In many cases, it just goes. You don't have to fight something that's already lost its grip.

I've seen it again and again—not just in my life, but in the lives of people I have prayed for. Someone is weighed down by decades of anger or rejection. We invite Jesus into the memory where that wound began. He speaks truth. The pain lifts. The person forgives. And then—sometimes before we even say *amen*—you can see it in their face: the heaviness is gone. They marvel at the feeling that something just lifted off of them. They've been delivered without showing signs of a single "manifestation."

That's why I believe emotional healing is one of the most powerful forms of deliverance available. It not only removes the enemy's access points; it restores the person's heart. And it leaves the believer not just free from harassment, but whole.

If you've ever been afraid of deliverance because it seemed scary or chaotic, I want you to know—it doesn't have to be that way. The Kingdom's authority is not in the volume of our voice, but in the presence of Jesus in the wound. When He heals the hurt, the darkness has no choice but to leave.

The Method

The method I use for emotional healing is simple, but effective. Anyone can learn it, and it doesn't require special training or seminary credentials. In fact, you can use it on yourself, or you can guide someone else through it—even from a distance. One friend of mine calls it *the one-minute healing prayer.*

Over the years, I've seen God use this process to bring freedom to people who have carried years of pain. It won't necessarily solve every type of mental illness or complex trauma, but it works well for the kind of emotional wounds most of us carry from life's difficult moments.

Before we get started, I want to offer a **note of caution**: If you've been diagnosed with Post Traumatic Stress Disorder (PTSD), Dissociative Identity Disorder (DID), or another condition that involves intense emotional triggers, please don't attempt this alone. Have someone you trust assist you—a friend, counselor, or prayer partner who understands your situation and can keep you safe if something surfaces that feels overwhelming.

The Core Steps

- Bring a painful memory to mind and pay attention to the strongest negative emotion you feel.

- Tell Jesus you want Him to remove the painful emotion from your soul.

- Ask Him to heal the wound in your soul caused by that emotion.

- Say out loud that you *receive* His healing.

- (Optional) Ask Him to replace the negative emotion with something positive. For example, "Lord, remove my anger and give me peace."

Working Through Layers

Once you've gone through those steps, bring the same memory to mind again. If you feel no negative emotion, you've been healed in that area. If a different emotion rises to the surface, you can simply repeat the process with that emotion. Keep going through each emotion until you can recall the event without feeling any negative emotions at all.

What If You Can't Remember the Event?

If you have memory gaps, you can ask the Holy Spirit to bring forgotten events to mind. As He does, focus on the emotions that come with them and walk through the same three steps. If you still can't remember a past event, that's okay—start with any negative emotions that are causing difficulty for you currently. Remember, Jesus is not healing the memories, He's healing the emotions.

A Life-Long Tool

You don't have to wait for a deep inner-healing session to use this. It's just as effective for the little hurts that happen every day:

Someone cuts you off in traffic, and anger spikes.

A coworker dismisses your idea, and you feel rejected.

A friend forgets to invite you to something, and you feel left out.

In the moment, give that painful emotion to Jesus and ask Him to heal the wound before it becomes a permanent scar.

The Forgiveness Factor

Harboring unforgiveness can open a door to demonic attack. Thus, forgiving those who have hurt you can help you live in peace. You don't have to forgive someone *before* you can receive emotional healing. Trying to forgive when you're still plagued with raw emotions can feel impossible. But once Jesus has removed those emotions, you may find it surprisingly easy to forgive—and even forget. Forgiveness does not mean the offending party is free of the consequences of their actions. It only means you will no longer be tormented by how others have treated you.

CHAPTER TWENTY-ONE

Spiritual Leadership

| *Denise's Perspective* |

I MADE A LIST OF qualities I wanted in a husband before I met Dave. One of the most important things on that list was that I wanted my husband to be the spiritual leader in our marriage. I also knew I didn't want a dictator, but a partner who would value my gifts, respect my calling, and lead with humility.

Some women are uncomfortable with the idea of male leadership (headship) because they've only seen it abused. But true biblical headship isn't about control. It's about the strength and security of knowing your spouse is praying for you, protecting you, and taking responsibility for the spiritual health of your home.

When Dave prays for me, I feel the difference. Peace settles in my spirit even in seasons of intense warfare. And when I pray for him in the Spirit, I know my words protect him.

Here's the balance: Dave leads, but I still have my voice. I recognize Dave's unique gifts, and he acknowledges mine as well. We often give deference to each other when a decision is clearly within the expertise of one or the other. He listens to my insights, and my perspective can often bring clarity to the situations we're facing. Sometimes, he'll prefer my perspective on an issue over his own and take action based on my understanding of the situation. Headship without domination allows us to make decisions together, but when a final decision has to be made, I trust him to hear God's voice and make a decision that is best for both of us. And because I trust him, he doesn't have to force his way—my respect allows him to lead with confidence.

We've learned that a marriage is strongest when both spouses are committed to lifting each other before God daily. Sometimes that means standing in agreement for a breakthrough. Sometimes it means praying for protection over each other's minds, health, and callings. And sometimes it means just thanking God for the gift you are to each other.

Marriage is a partnership under the umbrella of God's authority. When we live with that order in our hearts—without domination, without fear—there's a safety and strength that makes us nearly impossible for the enemy to divide.

Prayer Covering Model for Couples

If you're not accustomed to praying for (or with) your spouse, here are some simple ideas to get you started. Of course, you will expand on these and add more specifics as you deepen your prayer life.

Husband praying for wife:

"Father, I thank You for the gift of my wife. I ask You to cover her today with Your protection—mind, body, and spirit. Guard her from every attack of the enemy. Give her strength for the tasks ahead and Your peace that passes understanding. Remind her of her worth, her beauty, and her calling in You. I bless her today in the name of Jesus."

Wife praying for husband:

"Lord, I thank You for my husband and the calling You've placed on his life. Cover him with Your armor—protect his mind from lies, his body from harm, and his heart from discouragement. Give him wisdom, courage, and favor in every decision he makes today. Strengthen his faith, and remind him that he is deeply loved by You and by me. I bless him today in the name of Jesus."

Praying together:

"Father, we commit our marriage to You. Keep us united in heart, mind, and spirit. Make our home a place of peace, protection, and Your presence. Use us to accomplish Your purposes together. In Jesus' name, Amen."

CHAPTER TWENTY-TWO

Marital Unity in Spiritual Battles

| *Denise's perspective* |

YOU MIGHT BE SURPRISED TO learn that Dave and I have our most heated disagreements—not about money, schedules, or how to best cook a steak—but about editing books. You'd think that two people who work so closely together would glide through the process in perfect harmony, each one intuitively understanding the other's point of view. Not so. Our personalities and priorities clash most often when we are editing.

Dave's stake in a book is deeply personal. He spends months or years crafting the message, praying over the concepts, and making sure that every word reflects the heart of what he believes God is saying. To him, it's not just a book—it's a message God entrusted to him, and he feels the weight of stewarding it well. I see that, and I respect it. But my role in the process is different. My eyes are scanning for design flow, tone consistency, clarity of expression, and yes... legal liability. Those are the things that keep me awake at night. If something is written in a way that could be misunderstood, or if a statement could invite unnecessary trouble, I feel a responsibility to address it.

Sometimes our discussions get intense. Dave might feel that I'm "editing the heart" out of his message. I might think he's resisting changes that would make the book stronger and more effective. Both of us are trying to protect something important, but in the moment, it can feel like we're on opposing teams. And that's exactly where the enemy would love to keep us—believing the lie that we're adversaries instead of partners.

We've learned that in those moments, the first victory is simply to stop and remember the truth: we are on the same side. We share a common mission, and the only way to fulfill it effectively is to preserve our unity. When we pause long enough to truly listen, we begin to see the legitimacy in the other's concerns. Dave realizes that my goal isn't to dilute his message—it's to protect and amplify it so more people can hear and receive it. I realize that his passion for keeping the integrity of the content is as vital as my desire for clarity and professionalism.

This is where prayer becomes our reset button. One of us will have the clarity to push away from the computer, take a breath, and pray for unity. Asking God to help us dissolves the tension quickly. The sharp edges of frustration are softened. We may still see the issue differently, but we remember the bigger picture—God called us to this work together, and our unity is worth more than "winning" any argument.

Ephesians 4:3 says we are to be *"eager to maintain the unity of the Spirit in the bond of peace."* That word *eager* reminds me that unity doesn't happen by accident—it takes intentional effort. And it's not just about avoiding conflict; it's about guarding the spiritual bond that God has created between us. The enemy loves to use our differences, even our good intentions, to wedge us apart. However, when we recognize this, we can choose to view each disagreement not as a threat but as an opportunity to practice unity in the face of opposition.

You can turn the tables on the enemy in a heated moment if you stop, take your spouse's hand, and pray. Not a long, drawn-out prayer. Just a simple, "Lord, help us see each other through Your eyes. Protect our unity. Give us Your wisdom." That act alone sends a clear message to the enemy: you will not divide us.

When we find ourselves locking horns over an edit or a phrasing choice, I try to see it for what it really is: not just a creative disagreement, but a chance to choose unity over division. We may not agree on how to rewrite a sentence or paragraph, but we agree on this—God put us together for a purpose, and that purpose is worth protecting at all costs. And sometimes, that means setting the book aside, pouring two cups of coffee, and remembering that we're not just ministry partners or co-authors—we're a team, bound together by the Spirit, fighting the same fight, and called to walk in the bond of peace.

CHAPTER TWENTY-THREE

Healing Wounds and Restoring Trust

| *Dave's perspective* |

A COUPLE OF YEARS AGO, Denise and I had a serious disagreement—one of those rare but heavy ones that doesn't just blow over after a few hours. Usually, we're able to talk things through and find a resolution, but this time was different. Something about the way it unfolded left me feeling wounded in a deeper way, and instead of working through it right away, I pulled back. The resentment I felt lingered for more than a week. Now, I didn't give Denise the silent treatment to be mean or punish her. I simply didn't want to talk about it anymore. I told myself that avoiding the subject was a way to prevent another fight. But in reality, my avoidance was building a wall between us. Every day that passed, that wall grew a little taller—not because the disagreement was still fresh, but because we weren't reconnecting.

Time can soften the sharp edges of a wound, but I've learned that time by itself doesn't truly heal. Unresolved hurt has a way of hiding in the shadows, waiting for the next opportunity to come back to the surface. You can think you're fine until a similar situation happens, and suddenly, all that buried pain rushes back like it never left.

After several days, I realized I couldn't keep going like this. The distance between us felt unnatural and wrong. I knew I had to bring it before God. So, in the quiet of my own prayer time, I asked Him to heal the wound in my heart. I told Him exactly how I felt—no fancy words, no rehearsed speech. I asked Him to pull out the root of resentment that had taken hold and make room for love again. It wasn't an elaborate prayer, but it was honest.

Once I'd prayed, I knew what I had to do next. I went to Denise and apologized. I didn't defend myself or explain why I'd felt hurt. I didn't try to balance the scales by pointing out her part in the disagreement. I owned my part. I told her I was sorry for letting the hurt linger too long and for the wall it had created between us. She forgave me immediately, and in that moment, the wall crumbled. It was like turning on a light in a dark room. We moved forward as if the argument had never happened—not because we brushed it under the rug, but because forgiveness had closed the wound. That's the thing about forgiveness—it doesn't erase the past, but it removes the sting from it.

Forgiveness is one of the most potent weapons in the world. The enemy knows that a marriage divided is a marriage weakened. If he can keep two people replaying offenses in their minds, he can slowly erode their unity. But when we choose apology and forgiveness, we take away his ground.

Of course, forgiveness is only one part of it. Rebuilding trust takes time, and it's not a one-time decision—it's a process. It's choosing, moment by moment, to believe the best about your spouse, even when old insecurities try to whisper lies. It's speaking kindly, even when you could make a sharp remark. It's showing up, being present, and keeping your heart open.

When God is in the process, even a painful season can be a catalyst for deeper intimacy. What began as a wound can become a place of strength and unity in time. That's what happened to Denise and me. We were able to speak honestly about what emotions were at the root of the wound. We learned something about each other in that disagreement—not just what could hurt us, but what could heal us. And that understanding has made us stronger.

Colossians 3:13 says, *"Bear with each other and forgive one another if any of you has a grievance against someone. Forgive as the Lord forgave you."* I try to keep that in mind when I'm tempted to hold onto hurt. God's forgiveness toward me has been complete, free, and undeserved. How can I withhold the same from the person I love most?

If you've experienced hurt in your marriage, I encourage you—don't wait for time to fix it. Time doesn't heal wounds; God does. Take it to Him, let Him do the deep work, and then take the first step toward your spouse. You might be surprised at how quickly the wall can come down when forgiveness opens the door.

CHAPTER TWENTY-FOUR

Keeping Short Accounts

| *Dave's perspective* |

ONE OF THE BEST HABITS Denise and I have developed in our marriage could be called "keeping short accounts." It's the opposite of holding grudges. It means we don't let little offenses pile up until they turn into big problems. Early in our marriage, I didn't realize how easy it was to collect small grievances without even noticing. A sarcastic comment here. A forgotten errand there. A disagreement over something minor. On their own, these moments don't seem like much—but if you stack enough of them together without dealing with them, you eventually have a wall between you. And the higher the wall, the harder it is to see the other person clearly.

The Bible speaks to this principle in Ephesians 4:26–27: *"Do not let the sun go down while you are still angry, and do not give the devil a foothold."* That verse isn't just poetic advice—it's a spiritual safeguard. Unresolved anger is like an open door for the enemy to plant seeds of bitterness. Closing the door quickly keeps him from gaining ground in your marriage.

Keeping short accounts doesn't mean every disagreement gets resolved before bedtime. Sometimes it's late, emotions are high, and wisdom says, "Let's sleep on it and talk in the morning." But even in those cases, we make it a priority to say something like, "I love you. I'm still upset, but I'm committed to working this out." That way, the emotional connection remains, even if the details aren't resolved yet.

Here's what we've found helps keep our accounts short:

> **Address issues early.** The sooner you talk about a hurt or misunderstanding, the less chance it has to grow in your mind.

> **Use "I" statements.** Saying, "I felt hurt when..." is less likely to put your spouse on the defensive than saying, "You always..."

> **Don't stack offenses.** Deal with one situation at a time instead of pulling out a laundry list of every wrong from the past year.

I've noticed that when we live this way, the atmosphere in our home stays light. We can laugh more easily. We feel safe sharing our thoughts, even if they're different. The enemy has fewer opportunities to drive wedges between us.

Keeping short accounts is ultimately about valuing connection over being right. It's about saying, "I'd rather clear the air today than carry this into tomorrow." And when that becomes your normal rhythm, your marriage becomes a place where small offenses can't take root—because they never get the chance.

CHAPTER TWENTY-FIVE

Healing from Infidelity

| Dave's perspective |

INFIDELITY IS ONE OF THE most devastating blows a marriage can endure. It's not just the physical act of being unfaithful—it's the shattering of trust at the deepest level of intimacy. I've sat with friends who've been through it, and I've seen the hollow look in their eyes. I've also seen the tears of those who have been unfaithful, carrying the crushing weight of guilt and shame.

Whether it happens in the form of a physical affair, an emotional entanglement, or even a secret addiction, betrayal cuts us to the core because it touches what God designed marriage to protect—faithfulness, loyalty, and safety.

One reason it's so painful is that it attacks not just your trust in your spouse, but also your sense of worth. The betrayed spouse often finds themselves asking, *Wasn't I enough?* The enemy loves to pour lies into that wound—lies about your value, your attractiveness, and your future. But the truth is, infidelity says far more about the one who strayed than it does about the one who was betrayed. Still, that doesn't make the healing any easier.

If unfaithful behavior isn't confronted and stopped, it will sabotage a marriage beyond repair. But there is hope. God can make us faithful—not just in our outward actions, but in our thoughts, our desires, and even our emotional attachments. True faithfulness is more than the absence of cheating. It's the presence of a steadfast, unwavering commitment to your spouse, even when temptation comes knocking. That kind of loyalty doesn't happen by accident; it's cultivated over time, by surrendering your heart to God and allowing Him to shape your character.

When infidelity has occurred, both partners need healing—but that healing will look different for each person. For the betrayed spouse, it often means letting God tend to the wound that feels too raw to touch. It means allowing Him to rebuild the ability to trust again, to quiet the racing thoughts, and to restore a sense of worth and dignity that may have been trampled. For the one who strayed, it means genuine repentance—a turning away from the behavior and the conditions that led to it. It means embracing accountability, answering hard questions without defensiveness, and being patient with the pace of their spouse's healing.

Restoration is possible, but it's not a quick fix. It's a path that unfolds step by step, and every step requires humility, honesty, and grace. Early on, that might mean small but deliberate acts of rebuilding—keeping your word in little things, showing up when you say you will, opening your phone or your schedule without hesitation. It might mean inviting God into every conversation, asking Him to give you words that heal instead of words that reopen wounds.

For the betrayed, healing also means making a choice—not to excuse what happened, but to eventually release the offense into God's hands so it doesn't define your future. That doesn't mean trust is instantly restored. Trust is rebuilt the way a house is rebuilt after a fire—carefully, slowly, and with a strong foundation. But with God's help, it can stand again.

I've known couples whose marriages, after surviving infidelity, became stronger than they were before. Not because the betrayal was good—there's nothing good about sin—but because they invited God into the rubble. He took what was broken and made something new. They learned to communicate more honestly. They discovered a deeper compassion for one another's weaknesses. And their faith grew, because they saw firsthand that God can redeem even the most painful chapters of a marriage.

If you've been through the pain of infidelity, I want you to know this: it doesn't have to be the end of your story. With God's help, and with a shared commitment to the hard work of restoration, trust can be rebuilt. Your marriage may never look exactly as it did before—but that might be a good thing. It can grow into something richer, more honest, and more deeply rooted in grace.

Psalm 147:3 says, *"He heals the brokenhearted and binds up their wounds."* That promise isn't limited to individuals—it's for marriages too. And if God can raise the dead, He can breathe new life back into a relationship that feels beyond repair.

CHAPTER TWENTY-SIX

Avoiding Spiritual Mismatch

| *Denise's perspective* |

BEFORE WE MET, BOTH DAVE and I had been through marriages where
our spouses were either indifferent or averse to God. At the time, we
tried to make it work—we told ourselves that as long as we were faithful, committed, and responsible, the rest would fall into place. But the
truth is, when spouses hold opposing spiritual beliefs, it can slowly eat
away at the soul of a marriage. When one person pursues God with
passion while the other remains lukewarm or uninterested, it creates
a deep ache that no amount of surface-level compatibility can alleviate.

For those who are content to keep God on the sidelines, this arrangement might work. But for believers who burn with a desire to know
Him, follow Him, and experience His power, being bound to someone
who doesn't share that hunger is a recipe for heartbreak. You long for
shared prayer but find silence. You dream of worshiping together but
end up alone in the pew. You want to walk in step with the Spirit, but

instead you feel like you're dragging a weight that resists every stride forward. That was our story in our first marriages, and it left us determined never to repeat it.

That's why, when Dave and I came together, our shared foundation of faith was more than just a relief—it was a miracle. We believe in the same God and want the same things for our lives. That doesn't mean we see eye-to-eye on every subject. For example, some years ago, Dave stumbled across a new spiritual topic he was excited to explore—something I'd never even heard of before. Within days, he was itching to post about it online, to share what he was learning with others. I saw red flags. I hadn't had time to research it myself, and my instinct was to say, "Please, pump the brakes. Let's learn about this together before we start talking about it publicly."

That conversation was a small taste of what some couples deal with in much bigger ways. In our case, it was simply a matter of pacing and caution. But for other marriages, where spouses hold opposite views of God, it can feel like a much greater divide—especially when one spouse is walking closely with God and the other has little or no interest in Him at all.

I've talked with women who long for their husbands to lead spiritually but feel like they're walking alone. I've met husbands who ache for their wives to share their passion for miracles, but instead encounter indifference or resistance. When that's your reality, it's tempting to slip into either of two extremes: frustration that boils over into criticism, or resignation that quietly gives up hope. Neither one will draw your spouse closer to God.

What I've learned—even in our more minor disagreements—is that love without enabling is the key. That means you can set healthy boundaries about what you will and won't participate in, while still treating your spouse with kindness and respect. You can stand firm in your convictions without turning them into weapons. And you can pray for God to do in your spouse's heart what you cannot do by force of will.

1 Corinthians 7:16 poses an interesting question: *"How do you know, wife, whether you will save your husband? Or, how do you know, husband,*

whether you will save your wife?" It's not a command to pressure our spouse—it's a reminder that God is the one who changes hearts, not us. Our role is to live faithfully, speak truth with gentleness, and trust Him to do the rest.

When Dave and I find ourselves singing from different sheets of music, we work through it by listening to each other. We don't let differences of opinion turn into a wedge between us. Instead, we use it as a moment to practice mutual respect.

If you're in a marriage where the spiritual difference feels like a canyon rather than a crack, the principles are the same, just on a bigger scale. Submit the issue to God. Refuse to let bitterness take root. Celebrate the areas where you do agree, and keep your heart open for the Lord to move. And above all, remember that you are not alone—God is both your partner in prayer and the one who can bridge any divide.

Sometimes, unity comes from agreeing on the same doctrine. At other times, it comes from deciding to walk together in love, even before you see eye-to-eye. That, too, is a kind of victory—and it leaves room for God to do His best work.

CHAPTER TWENTY-SEVEN

Conflict Without Carnage

| *Dave's perspective* |

I'VE BEEN IN RELATIONSHIPS WHERE it seemed like the other person was always looking for a reason to start a fight. It rarely mattered what I said or did—there was this constant undercurrent of tension, as if we were one wrong word away from an explosion. You constantly feel like you're walking on eggshells. You watch every syllable, tiptoe around every opinion, and still somehow manage to set off a land mine you didn't even see.

That's one of the reasons I'm grateful for Denise. She's what the Bible calls "a person of peace." Her natural gentleness and quiet spirit make it easy to be around her. That doesn't mean we never disagree—we do. But our disagreements don't usually turn into wars. There's no scoreboard, no winner-takes-all attitude. We typically settle things quickly, and even in the middle of a heated moment, I never feel like she's out to hurt me.

Over the years, we've both learned that fighting fair isn't just a relationship skill—it's a spiritual discipline. The enemy loves to take a slight misunderstanding and blow it out of proportion into a major offense. He thrives on escalation. That's why one of the most vital things we can do as a couple is to defuse a disagreement before it turns into carnage. Sometimes that means lowering our voices or taking a break from the conversation until emotions cool down. And sometimes, it's choosing to listen without loading the next verbal round in the chamber.

Proverbs 15:1 says, *"A gentle answer turns away wrath, but a harsh word stirs up anger."* I've frequently seen that play out in real time. If Denise responds with gentleness when I'm frustrated, it's like slapping an ice pack on a burn—it just stops the heat from building. And when I choose to do the same for her, the conversation stays constructive instead of destructive.

The wise approach to problem-solving is focusing on the issue instead of attacking each other. It's easy to get sidetracked into old grievances, but dragging out the history book rarely helps. We've made it a point to deal with what's in front of us, not rehash everything from the last five years.

I'm not saying we've perfected this. There are still moments when one of us says something sharper than we intended. But when that happens, we own it and apologize quickly. That simple habit—quick apologies and quick forgiveness—has probably saved us from more damage than we realize.

Conflict is inevitable in marriage. Carnage is not. If you can learn to fight fair, to keep your words measured, your hearts soft, and your focus on solving the problem instead of scoring points, you'll find that even your disagreements can become opportunities to grow closer.

CHAPTER TWENTY-EIGHT

Resetting the Atmosphere

| *Denise's perspective* |

ONE OF THE MOST IMPORTANT lessons I've learned is that atmosphere matters. You can't always see it, but you can feel it—the tension in the room, the unspoken words hanging in the air, the heaviness that makes you want to avoid eye contact. It's more than just a mood; it's the spiritual climate of your relationship in that moment. It's a matter of situational awareness—the recognition that your environment has changed. And if that climate is left unchecked, it can begin to harden your heart toward your spouse without you even realizing it.

Over the years, I've come to recognize those subtle shifts. Maybe Dave's shoulders are tight and his tone a little short. Maybe I'm feeling defensive and not sure why. It's in those moments that I've learned to act quickly—not to suppress my feelings, but to guard the peace of our home. If I sense that we're drifting toward that heavy, disconnected space, I've made it a habit to reset the atmosphere before it takes root.

That doesn't mean pretending everything is fine or sweeping issues under the rug. It means making a deliberate choice about the spirit (attitude) in which we approach each other. We may not agree on everything—no couple does—but we've both decided that peace is worth protecting. That decision shapes how I respond when tension rises. My first instinct isn't to push back with equal force, because I know that will only add fuel to the fire. Instead, I try to lower my voice, soften my words, and remind myself that my goal isn't to win an argument—it's to win back the connection.

The reset of the atmosphere sometimes comes through a gentle word at just the right time. When Dave senses an undesirable change in the atmosphere, he'll sometimes crack a joke that reframes the issue we're discussing, and changes the mood. Other times, it's best to say nothing at all until emotions settle. There are even moments when I'll change the subject temporarily or suggest we take a short break—because I've learned that cooling the temperature is not avoidance; it's wisdom. Proverbs 17:14 says, *"Starting a quarrel is like breaching a dam; so drop the matter before a dispute breaks out."* That verse isn't telling us to ignore problems—it's telling us to know when to step back so the floodwaters don't sweep away the relationship in the process.

I've also found that small gestures can shift the atmosphere in ways words can't. Thanking Dave for something he did, offering a smile, or reaching for his hand when we're walking through a store—those simple acts can be like opening a window to let fresh air into a stuffy room. They say, *"We're still us. This is still home. I still choose you."*

But resetting the atmosphere is about more than just conflict management—it's about spiritual protection. The tone of our home sets the stage for God's presence. When peace is guarded, it creates space for Him to dwell there. And when His presence fills the atmosphere, something beautiful happens: healing becomes easier, understanding flows more naturally, and unity begins to grow again.

There will always be moments of tension. But the atmosphere of your marriage doesn't have to be at the mercy of circumstances or emotions. With God's help, you can choose to set the tone—and in doing so, you protect not only your peace, but the sacred space where love can flourish.

CHAPTER TWENTY-NINE

The Bridge Back

| *Dave's perspective* |

IN EVERY MARRIAGE, MOMENTS WILL occur when the closeness you normally feel is out of reach. That distance may be caused by a sharp word said in frustration, a misunderstanding that snowballs into something bigger, or a difference in perspective on a major issue. It can happen after multiple long, busy days when life pulls you in separate directions. The point is, the gap will come. The real test of a marriage isn't whether you can avoid conflict—it's whether—and how quickly you can find your way back to each other.

Because I'm susceptible to pride, for me, the bridge back usually begins with humility. I swallow my pride, acknowledge Denise's perspective, admit that I went too far, and affirm that the relationship matters more than being right. Even in cases where I'm convinced that I am "right," being vindicated is a hollow victory if it leaves me disconnected from Denise. If we're discussing an issue that has no objective right or wrong position, it's wise not to insist that your view is superior to that of another. The tone I choose in these cases can close the relational gap or make it wider. If I want to strengthen my bond with Denise, I have to choose gentleness—even when my pride would rather keep arguing.

Reconciling with an estranged person rarely occurs in a single, giant leap. More often, it's built through small steps. Sometimes it's an honest apology, spoken without excuses. Other times, it's something as simple as a soft touch on her shoulder, asking if she'd like me to make more coffee, or sending her a quick message to say, *"I love you."* These aren't bribes for forgiveness—they're signals that my heart is moving toward her again. I've found that these small, intentional gestures often melt the ice faster than hours of explanation or debate ever could.

And it's not just about action—it's about patience. There have been moments when I felt ready to reconnect, but Denise needed a little more time to process. That's okay. Building the bridge back means starting from your side, taking a step, and waiting for the other person to take theirs. You can't force someone to meet you in the middle, but you can make it easier for them to want to.

Over time, something beautiful happens. The gap that felt so wide yesterday begins to shrink. The awkward silence fades, giving way to conversation and laughter. The distance becomes a memory—one that actually strengthens your bond, because you know you can weather the storm and still come back together.

Every couple faces these moments. The key is deciding—every single time—that the connection you share is worth more than the argument you won, the point you proved, or the pride you protected. That choice, made again and again, keeps the bridge between you strong enough to carry you through anything.

CHAPTER THIRTY

Intimacy on Every Level

| *Dave's perspective* |

PHYSICAL INTIMACY IS PERHAPS THE easiest part of marriage. Even couples who seem to be in constant conflict can sometimes call a truce long enough for a few minutes of romance. But if a marriage is built *only* on physical connection, it won't last. Real intimacy goes deeper. Emotional closeness and spiritual oneness are what give physical love its depth and meaning, and those don't happen automatically. They must be nurtured, protected, and cultivated over time. Emotional intimacy can be the trickiest of the three. We all carry invisible "land mines" in our hearts—old wounds, insecurities, or buried fears—that can detonate unexpectedly in a conversation. At times, I don't even realize I've stepped on one until Denise goes quiet, or I find myself reacting more strongly than the situation warrants. When that happens, it's easy to shut down or retreat, but I've learned that's the moment to lean in. Emotional intimacy is built by making it safe for your spouse to share without fear of being dismissed, criticized, or punished for their honesty. That kind of safety takes time to create, and it can be destroyed if we're careless with our words or tone.

Thankfully, there's a remedy for those emotional land mines—emotional healing. We've both experienced how Jesus can step into a painful memory and lift away the hurt, replacing it with peace. Every time that happens, another wall comes down, and it's easier to be transparent with each other. That transparency is the soil where emotional intimacy grows.

Then there's spiritual intimacy, which is the most profound connection of all. For us, it's two people committing to God's plan and following His lead. This means praying together regularly—about everything from our work to our friendships to our dreams for the future. It also means sharing what we're learning individually. Sometimes Denise will tell me about something God spoke to her while she was painting. Other times, I'll share a dream I feel has spiritual significance, and together we'll discern its meaning. These moments draw us closer not just to each other, but to God Himself.

Here's what I've learned: the closer we each get to God, the closer we get to each other. Picture a triangle—God is at the top, and each of us is on one of the bottom corners. As we move toward Him, we move toward each other. When we neglect our spiritual connection, we drift apart—not because we've stopped loving each other, but because we're no longer moving toward the same center.

If there are obstacles in the way of intimacy—whether physical, emotional, or spiritual—they need to be addressed, not ignored. Sometimes that means having hard conversations. Sometimes it's getting help from a trusted mentor, pastor, or counselor. And sometimes it simply means slowing down long enough to notice where you've grown distant and making the intentional choice to come together again.

A healthy marriage is one where intimacy exists on every level—physical affection, emotional safety, and spiritual unity. When all three are in place, your connection becomes a fortress. The storms of life can beat against it, but it will stand, because it's anchored in love that's more than just a feeling—it's a covenant built in the presence of God.

CHAPTER THIRTY-ONE

Trust and Intimacy

| *Denise's perspective* |

THIS CHAPTER MAY SEEM A bit heavy to read. Nevertheless, I include these stories to illustrate that even if your past is marred by trauma—which could negatively affect intimacy in marriage—emotional healing can help you begin again.

Early Trauma

When I was 19 years old, a disturbed man held me and my art school roommate at knifepoint to force us into sexual acts. It turned into a four-hour ordeal of fear. Thankfully, we escaped without *physical* wounds. My roommate, who had a history of childhood sexual abuse, wanted to stay silent and bury it internally, as had been her customary response to traumas in her past. I was determined to convince her that we both needed to report the incident to the police so he couldn't harm anyone else. After much pleading, she agreed, and the city prosecutors opened up a criminal case.

What followed was almost as punishing as the assault itself. We had to retell our story again and again—to police, prosecutors, counselors, and even friends—reliving the trauma each time. We jumped at every knock on our apartment door, a sound that became a trigger. The case dragged on for years and ended with a plea deal that resulted in the man serving only a fraction of the original jail time.

Betrayed Trust

In my previous marriage, years before I met Dave, I faced another kind of violation—different in form, but similar in the way it undermined trust. I discovered something that broke my heart—a secret addiction that my ex-husband hid from me for more than a decade. I couldn't believe it, at first—maybe it was just a mistake or a passing temptation. But as the truth unfolded, I realized it was an entrenched habit that had grown, quietly eroding my trust in my then-husband's fidelity to our marriage vows. The sense of betrayal was overwhelming by the time I finally confronted it. I felt deceived, unwanted, and humiliated. Eventually, despite counseling, the damage became too great to repair, and the marriage ended.

Coming to terms with that reality was a long, painful process. Closing that chapter of my life was anything but easy. The wounds did not simply vanish with time. For years, I carried the weight of inadequacy and shame, questioning whether I had played some role in what happened. However, the truth is that I was deceived. From the very beginning, he knew where I stood on pornography, yet he chose to hide it from me—successfully—for years.

What is so often dismissed as a private habit or a victimless act was, in my experience, an unwelcome intruder that eroded the foundation of trust in my marriage. I began to question not only his fidelity but also the stories that explained his late nights and disinterest in attending family holiday events with me. To me, pornography does not remain contained in secrecy; it seeps into the marriage, distorting love into performance, fueling unrealistic expectations, and replacing genuine intimacy with a shallow imitation.

Seek Healing

Yet God, in His mercy, did not leave me there. The enemy caused those traumas, but God flipped the tables and used the experiences for my good—to help me seek Him. After accepting Christ and learning of His forgiveness, I was finally able to forgive the perpetrator of the trauma I suffered at age 19. A short time later, I released the victim label I had silently carried for two decades. Over time, I came to see my ex-husband through a more compassionate lens. I know certain wounds cut deeply, especially when inflicted by someone you assumed you could trust.

Many people carry traumas like mine—or much worse. For some couples, the obstacle to intimacy isn't a current sin, but the lingering effects of past abuse or betrayal. Those wounds can make it hard to be fully present with your spouse, even years later. If that's your story, I'd like to encourage you: God can heal those wounds. I've experienced His restoration myself. It took prayer, honesty, some solid counseling from a couple of trusted pastors, and a willingness to let God heal the wounded parts of my soul. Little by little, He replaced the shame with a sense of worth and my relationship fears with peace.

If you've been wounded in this area, please know this: God's plan for intimacy is not one of shame, fear, or avoidance. It's meant to be a safe, joyful expression of love between husband and wife—a place where both are cherished, seen, and known. With His help, intimacy in marriage can be a place of healing instead of hurt, a source of unity instead of division, and a reflection of the covenant love that God designed from the very beginning.

Beginning Again

When I met Dave and we got married, I experienced what it meant to begin again. We knew one thing for certain: we would guard our marriage intimacy from intrusions. We would commit to protecting the physical, emotional, and spiritual bond God had given us in marriage. I recommend creating some common-sense ground rules.

Here are some suggestions to build trust and closeness:

- Use emotional healing to free yourself from the triggers formed during trauma.

- Refuse to let anything—including past trauma—invade the sacred marriage relationship.

- Learn each other's boundaries and respect them.

- Never use sex as a weapon or bargaining chip.

- Go to bed at the same time together, if possible.

- Keep television out of the bedroom—it is a distraction.

- Avoid opposite-sex "best friends" or "just friends" who might have romantic intentions if given the chance.

If you're reading this book, you're seeking change. Everyone has had their trust broken in some way. But God can heal your wounds, help you trust again, and enable you to enjoy intimacy with your spouse.

CHAPTER THIRTY-TWO

Sabbath and Rest

| *Dave's perspective* |

THE SABBATH IS NOT A rule we must keep in order to stay in God's good graces. It's an invitation—a reminder that rest is not a luxury, it's a necessity. I like to think of it as a strategic move in spiritual warfare. The enemy loves to see us worn down, stretched thin, and running on fumes. A tired soul is easier to discourage, easier to tempt, and easier to divide from others. But a rested soul is far harder to defeat.

I've always had a workaholic streak. When I love what I'm doing— whether it's writing, researching, or editing—I can lose track of time completely. Before I know it, I've been at my desk for twelve hours straight, barely looking up from the screen. At first, it feels productive. But eventually, the fatigue catches up. My creativity dries up. My patience shortens. And the people I love most start to feel like they're competing with my work for attention. That's when I realize I'm overdue for a reset. For us, the Sabbath isn't about taking a specific day off—it's about creating a rhythm of refreshment. Sometimes Denise and I will turn off our phones, go for a drive, or sit on the couch and just talk. Other times, we might go for a long walk, read for pleasure instead of research, or linger after breakfast without rushing to the next thing. The goal is intentionally shifting the focus from doing to being.

We probably don't unplug as often as we need to. Our work keeps us busy with deadlines—even on weekends. But one of the best things about practicing rest together is how it deepens our connection. When we slow down, we notice beautiful things we would have rushed past—a pair of birds perched on a plant in the backyard, the sound of our spouse's laughter, or the way moonlight reflects off the pool. Those moments are where intimacy grows, and they're often the first thing to vanish when life gets too busy.

Jesus modeled rest for us. Even in the middle of crowds and urgent needs, He would withdraw to the solitude of the mountains to pray. He didn't rest because He was lazy—He rested because it was essential to finishing His mission. If the Son of God made space for stillness, how much more should we?

Rest is a form of trust. When we set aside our to-do lists and let the world keep spinning without our help, we're saying, "God, I believe You can handle it." And in marriage, rest says, "I value you more than I value my productivity." That's why the Sabbath isn't just about refreshing ourselves—it's about protecting our unity.

When Denise and I embrace a rhythm of rest, we're not just avoiding burnout. We're building resilience. We're choosing to allow space for peace in our home. And every time we do, we find that rest doesn't make us fall behind—it makes us stronger for whatever comes next.

CHAPTER THIRTY-THREE

Serving God in Different Ways

| Denise's perspective |

THE FARTHEST THING FROM MY mind when I became a believer was to do typical work in "women's ministry." I didn't picture myself hosting women's Bible studies, speaking at conferences, or fitting the mold of the perfect Proverbs 31 woman. Honestly, I felt I had too many flaws to be useful in roles like that. My picture of what God could do through me was smaller, perhaps shaped by my introverted personality, and my tendency to compare my skills to the talents of others. But God doesn't seem to be concerned about the things I think disqualify me. He sees the gifts He placed inside me before I was even born, and He knows how to use them—sometimes in ways I never imagined.

For example, my background as a secular vocalist prepared me to use my voice for worship in my Pennsylvania church, and again later in Washington State. I'm grateful God gave me a way to serve that ideally suited me. Serving God should not be like trying to fit a round peg into a square hole. Rather, it should feel natural to us. It may be expressed as something we do as a career, but in a modified form.

Here's something we could contemplate: Did God pair me with Dave because I worked as a graphic designer for a book publisher? He wanted Dave to write—and he knew I would help and encourage him. My calling doesn't look like Dave's, and that's not supposed to be the case. While he's in his element speaking to groups, writing books, and praying with people, I often serve quietly behind the scenes—editing a manuscript, organizing details, or creating artwork in my studio. The beauty of it is, God can take all of it, whether public or private, and use it for His Kingdom.

In the past, I would see Dave's passion for ministry and think that because I wasn't doing exactly the same work, I was somehow less spiritual or less important to God's plan. But over time, the Lord showed me that different callings don't compete with each other—they complement each other. When we both lean into the strengths and assignments God has given us, our marriage becomes a more complete picture of His heart.

Serving God in different ways means learning to cheer each other on without feeling threatened or left behind. It's recognizing that in some seasons, one of us will be in the spotlight while the other is supporting from the shadows. And then the roles might switch. Both positions matter, and both require humility. If Dave is finishing up a book manuscript, I'll make the house as quiet as I can so he can focus. When I immerse myself in a big creative project, he'll pick up extra household responsibilities without complaining.

Resentment can creep into a marriage if one spouse feels their work is undervalued or ignored. The antidote is gratitude—choosing to see and appreciate the ways in which your spouse serves, even if those ways look nothing like your own. I may not be in the spotlight with Dave, but when someone tells me how much his writing helped them, I know that my quiet editing work played a role in that, too. And when he thanks me for creating beauty and order in our home, it reminds me that my contributions matter to him just as much as his matter to me.

At the end of the day, serving God in different ways is less about what we do and more about *how* we do it—together, with joy, without comparison, and with the shared goal of glorifying Him. When we keep that perspective, our differences don't divide us. They make us stronger.

CHAPTER THIRTY-FOUR

The Prophetic in Marriage

| *Dave's perspective* |

I RECEIVE A LOT OF unusual dreams. Some are literal. Others are vivid and symbolic, and still others are strange enough that I have to sit with them for a while before I even know if they mean anything. Sometimes they're encouraging. Other times they're warnings. And occasionally, they make me want to spring into action immediately. Early in our marriage, I occasionally made the mistake of running with a dream without telling Denise first. My intentions were good—I wanted to be obedient to God—but zeal without wisdom can create unnecessary problems.

As I've matured, I've discovered that God rarely asks me to act on something immediately. He nearly always gives us enough lead time to process the dream, pray over it, and confirm its meaning. And that word "us" is important. Denise is an essential part of the process. God gave me a wife whose instincts are sharp and whose spiritual radar is tuned in, even if she doesn't always see herself that way.

There have been times I've come to her with a dream. I'd lay it all out—every detail, every possible interpretation. She'd listen quietly, and then she'd ask a simple question or point out something I hadn't considered. Sometimes, her insight has confirmed what I sensed. Other times, she's helped me realize I was misreading the dream entirely. Those conversations have saved us from wasted time, unnecessary stress, and the embarrassment of acting on something half-baked.

Scripture gives us a clear framework for handling prophetic revelation. First Thessalonians 5:20–21 says, *"Do not despise prophecies, but test everything; hold fast what is good."* That means we don't ignore or dismiss what God might be saying, but we also don't accept it blindly. We weigh it against scripture. We pray. We seek confirmation. And in marriage, that confirmation often comes through the spouse God has given us.

Denise and I have learned to treat dreams and prophetic impressions as invitations, not instructions. An invitation to pray. An invitation to listen. An invitation to wait until the timing and the interpretation are clear. Acting too quickly can cause unnecessary harm. Acting in unity, after prayer and agreement, brings peace—even if the message is challenging.

We've also learned that prophetic guidance isn't always for immediate action. Sometimes God shows us something months or even years ahead of time so we'll be prepared when the moment comes. In those cases, having both of us on the same page makes it much easier to recognize the moment when it arrives.

Prophetic revelation is a gift, but like all gifts from God, it has to be stewarded well. When we interpret dreams and words together, we not only grow in spiritual discernment—we grow in trust with each other. And that unity becomes its own form of protection. It ensures that when we do act, we act as one, walking in step with the Spirit and with each other.

CHAPTER THIRTY-FIVE

Hospitality as a Couple

| *Denise's perspective* |

I'M AN INTROVERT BY NATURE. That doesn't mean I don't like people—it just means I recharge in quiet times, often alone, and social interaction can drain me if I'm not careful. Dave is the opposite. He thrives in a crowd, comes alive in conversation, and seems to draw energy from every handshake and story exchanged. Early in our marriage, we discovered just how different our social rhythms were.

American psychologist David Keirsey wrote a book about personality types titled *Please Understand Me*. When we took his online temperament assessment, we learned that our personality types are considered "ideal mates." And in many ways, that's proven to be true. Dave's social activities and ministry gatherings tend to keep me from becoming a hermit. I, in turn, help him avoid the burnout that extroverts sometimes experience when they overcommit. It's a balance that took time to recognize and develop, but now it feels natural.

Hospitality, for us, isn't about throwing Pinterest-worthy dinner parties or having a perfectly curated home—although I *do* try to bring my design skills into our rooms. It's about opening our door—and our lives—in a way that makes people feel welcomed, loved, and safe. Sometimes it's hosting friends for coffee. Other times, it's inviting someone who's struggling to join us for a meal. We've had small gatherings around our dining table that turned into deep spiritual conversations and moments of prayer we'll never forget.

Romans 12:13 says, *"Contribute to the needs of the saints and seek to show hospitality."* When someone steps into our home, we want them to feel the peace of God in the atmosphere. We want them to leave more encouraged than when they arrived.

That said, hospitality without boundaries can lead to exhaustion. We've learned that "yes" isn't always the most loving answer—especially if it means saying "no" to the health of our marriage. If I agree to host when I'm already depleted, my attitude and energy will affect the tone of the evening. Likewise, if Dave pushes himself to entertain when he's already stretched thin, the joy of hospitality disappears. So we set limits. We agree together on how many gatherings we'll host in a given season. We block out nights just for ourselves. And we've learned to listen to the Holy Spirit about whom to invite, when to open our home, and when to rest instead.

Hospitality as a couple isn't just about the guests—it's about the two of you working together in unity. Dave's strengths and my strengths are different, but when we combine them, the result is something neither of us could offer alone. He brings warmth, enthusiasm, and connection. I bring attention to detail, an eye for creating a peaceful environment, and a sense of when it's time to wrap things up.

In the end, hospitality isn't just what happens in our home—it's the spirit in which we offer our lives. Whether it's at our dining table, in a coffee shop, or during a conversation on our back patio, our goal is the same: to make space for people to experience God's love.

CHAPTER THIRTY-SIX

Navigating Seasons of Change

| *Dave's perspective* |

WHEN WE MOVED TO ARIZONA in 2011, I assumed I'd continue working as a paramedic until I was too old to push a gurney. It seemed like the safe, sensible plan for someone like me. After all, I'd been in emergency medical services for thirty-five years. I knew the job, its routines, and the demands. I'm a person of habit, and I hate when my routines are changed—even routines that cause frustration. What I didn't realize was that the career I had once loved was slowly draining the life out of me.

Eventually, the cracks began to show. My managers were more concerned with optics and cash flow than with people. Our dispatchers were relentless, stacking one call on top of another with no regard for how late I'd get home. Most days, I would come home several hours past the end of my 12-hour shift, physically spent and emotionally drained. I began to resent the management and the very work that had once given me a sense of purpose.

Somewhere in that frustration, I found myself drawn to writing. At first, it was just a creative outlet—a way to process my thoughts after long shifts. But the more I wrote, the more alive I felt. It was as if God was quietly planting the seeds of a new calling while I was still holding on tightly to the old one.

Then Denise said something that stopped me in my tracks: "I think you should put all those social media stories you've been writing into a book." My first thought was: *That's crazy.* Writing books wasn't a real job. Not one that could pay the bills, anyway. Then she took it a step further: "I know how to start a business."

That idea terrified me. I had always worked for someone else. I never wanted the weight of running a business, managing the finances, or being solely responsible for whether it succeeded or failed. But God has a way of leading us where we never thought we'd go—one small step at a time.

We didn't leap into change overnight. We prayed. We talked through every detail. We took small, manageable steps toward the future God was showing us. Not knowing if we could succeed, I kept working my shifts while writing in my spare time. Denise was working from home as a freelance graphic designer and photo editor. We sat together at the computer on endless nights and weekends, editing and formatting our work. We learned the steps to self-publishing slowly, through an online course that provided a step-by-step plan. We said "yes" only when we both felt peace about the next step.

We made a gradual transition to help me leave my paramedic job with the goal of writing and publishing full-time. Today, we own a small company and lead a nonprofit ministry together. Looking back, I can see God's fingerprints on every part of the transition. He didn't shove us into change—He guided us. And I believe that's the key to staying connected in seasons of uncertainty: move at the pace of peace.

Isaiah 30:21 says, *"Whether you turn to the right or to the left, your ears will hear a voice behind you, saying, 'This is the way; walk in it.'"* That's what it felt like—God quietly confirming each decision until the path ahead was clear.

Change will come for every couple—sometimes by choice, sometimes by circumstance. The real question is whether you'll face it together or drift apart in the process. For us, staying connected meant talking openly about our fears, listening to each other's concerns, and refusing to take a step until we both sensed God's leading.

Transitions can be terrifying, but they can also strengthen your marriage. When you walk through changes side by side, you emerge not just with a new chapter in your life—but with a deeper bond that can weather whatever comes next.

CHAPTER THIRTY-SEVEN

Purpose as a Couple

| *Denise's perspective* |

THERE'S A SPECIAL KIND OF blessing that comes when two people choose to work together in unity—not just for their own benefit, but for the good of their family, their community, and God's kingdom. Marriage isn't meant to be a private, self-contained arrangement. When God brings two people together, He's thinking about more than their happiness. He's thinking about the impact their partnership will have on the world around them. I've seen it firsthand in our own home. When Dave and I are in sync, everything runs smoother. There's peace in the atmosphere. Decisions feel lighter because we carry them together. Even our disagreements, when handled well, seem to strengthen us instead of pulling us apart. That unity doesn't just bless us—it spills over into the lives of those who interact with us.

If you have children, your unity is one of the greatest gifts you can give them. A home filled with mutual respect, affection, and shared purpose creates an atmosphere where they can grow without the constant fear of conflict. They watch how you speak to each other, how you solve problems, how you celebrate and grieve together. Those patterns take root in their hearts and will one day shape how they approach their own relationships. When you raise children in unity, you're not just influencing the present—you're shaping the future. But your influence doesn't stop there. Whether you realize it or not, other couples are watching you. Friends, coworkers, neighbors, and even casual acquaintances notice when a marriage is healthy, supportive, and purposeful. They may never say a word about it, but the way you live can inspire them to believe that deep, lasting love is still possible. In a world that often treats marriage as a disposable commodity, a couple that loves well becomes a powerful testimony to God's character.

For Dave and me, part of our mission is encouraging other couples. Sometimes that happens through a book we've written. Other times, it's opening our home, sharing a meal, or listening when someone needs to talk. Purpose doesn't necessarily imply a public ministry. It can be personal—as simple as showing up consistently in love.

Years ago, a mobile notary public stopped by our home and brought a stack of documents. While signing, we engaged her in conversation. Somehow, we ended up discussing how God brought us together—and she shared about her live-in boyfriend who wanted her to marry him. He kept asking, and she kept turning him down. She was a bit unhappy with some of his traits, but it was nothing major—she admitted that she was looking for perfection and that he was, in fact, a good man. We encouraged her, and after four hours of talking at our kitchen table, we both hugged her, and she left.

I believe it was months later when an unexpected and exciting thing happened. Our notary friend emailed Dave to tell us that she and her boyfriend had just gotten married in Las Vegas. She went on to thank us and say that our marriage story inspired her to say "yes."

Early in our marriage, we considered hosting marriage workshops. That idea didn't materialize in the way we had envisioned at the time, but we have always had the shared mission to see marriages thrive. Dave's strengths are different from mine, and our callings sometimes take us in different directions. But when we bring those differences under the same mission—to honor God and bless others—they don't compete. They complement.

So whether your purpose together is raising godly children, serving in a ministry, building a business, or simply living in a way that reflects Christ's love, guard your unity. Protect it, because when a couple is united in purpose, they become more than the sum of their parts— they become a light that draws others toward hope, healing, and the heart of God.

Romans 15:5–6 says, *"May the God who gives endurance and encouragement give you the same attitude of mind toward each other that Christ Jesus had, so that with one mind and one voice you may glorify the God and Father of our Lord Jesus Christ."*

CHAPTER THIRTY-EIGHT

Standing Together, Moving Forward

| *From both of us* |

WHEN WE LOOK BACK ON our story, what stands out isn't just the lessons we learned or the battles we faced. What we remember is God's faithfulness. He has carried us through storms, taught us through our mistakes, and blessed us in ways we could never have orchestrated ourselves. If this book has shown you anything, we pray it has shown you this: a marriage rooted in Christ is not fragile—it is resilient.

We've walked through seasons of loss, of blended family challenges, of spiritual warfare, and of financial strain. Each of those moments could have driven us apart. But instead, as we chose to seek God together, they became stepping stones that drew us closer—not just to each other, but to Him. The same can be true for you.

Marriage is not about two perfect people fitting seamlessly together. It's about two imperfect people learning how to love, forgive, and stand shoulder to shoulder under God's banner of grace. That's why prayer matters. That's why unity matters. That's why guarding your marriage against the schemes of the enemy matters. Because your marriage is more than a private relationship—it's a testimony of what God can do when two become one.

So where do you go from here? Start small. Choose one thing you can do today that says to your spouse, *"We are on the same team."* Maybe that's praying a short prayer together. Maybe it's speaking words of encouragement instead of criticism. Maybe it's choosing to pause and listen instead of reacting. Small acts, performed consistently, can change the entire atmosphere of a home.

And don't be afraid of setbacks. Every couple has them. The victory isn't in never stumbling—the victory is in getting back up together, dusting yourselves off, and continuing forward. God's mercies are new every morning, and that includes His mercies for your marriage.

> *Our prayer for you is that you never face battles alone, but always stand side by side; that you find joy not only in life's milestones but in the simple, everyday moments; that you learn to recognize God's gentle whispers as clearly as you hear each other's voices; and that, through it all, you come to see your marriage not only as a precious gift, but as a sacred calling that you accomplish together.*

We don't claim to have all the answers. What we do know is this: the same God who sustained us will sustain you. He delights in your marriage. He is for your unity. And when you choose to invite Him into the center of your relationship, He will do more than strengthen your bond—He will use your love as a light for others.

ABOUT THE AUTHOR

Praying Medic is a former atheist who has worked as a paramedic for decades. After having a dramatic encounter in which God told him He would use him to heal the sick, he began praying with his patients and with strangers, and has seen thousands of them healed. He began writing about his life as a medic in 2009, published his first book in 2013, and has since written over twenty books, spanning both fiction and non-fiction, on topics such as faith, spirituality, preparedness, and off-grid communication. His books have inspired thousands of readers to seek God for themselves. Known to friends as Dave, he's also a public speaker, teacher, and podcaster. He lives in sunny Arizona with his wife, Denise, a painter and graphic designer.

For all titles visit: PrayingMedic.com

New! Science Fiction

The Red Sky Trilogy

• Opturius: Beneath a Crimson Sky

Beneath a crimson sky on a distant world, a broken man dares to climb toward the unknown...

After a tragic accident leaves Adam Walker guilt-ridden and adrift, he wants nothing more than to disappear. But life has other plans. Abducted by an interstellar team and taken to the planet Opturius, Adam is asked to do the one thing he no longer believes he can.

For fans of **C.S. Lewis**, **Ursula K. Le Guin**, and **Richard Powers**, *Opturius* is a lyrical, soul-stirring journey across an alien world—where a lone climber meets the divine.

Blending spiritual depth, poetic prose, and cosmic mystery, this is science fiction for seekers—for those who believe stories should move your heart and mind.

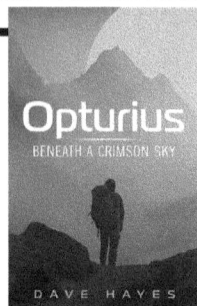

The Kingdom of God Made Simple

• Divine Healing Made Simple
• Seeing in the Spirit Made Simple
• Hearing God's Voice Made Simple
• Traveling in the Spirit Made Simple
• Dream Interpretation Made Simple
• Power and Authority Made Simple
• Emotional Healing Made Simple

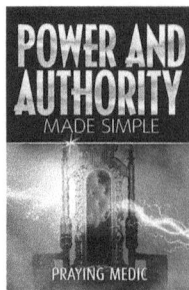

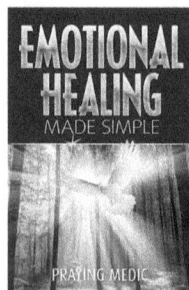

The Courts of Heaven

- Defeating Your Adversary in the Court of Heaven
- Operating in the Court of Angels

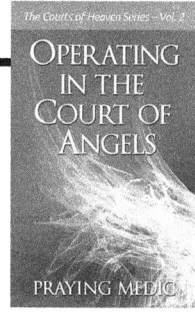

My Craziest Adventures with God

- My Craziest Adventures with God - Vol. 1
- My Craziest Adventures with God - Vol. 2

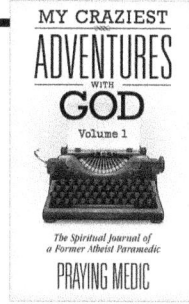

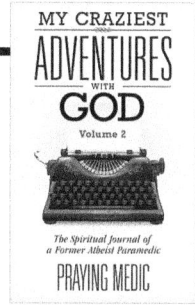

The Gates of Shiloh (novel series)

- The Gates of Shiloh
- Charity's Garden

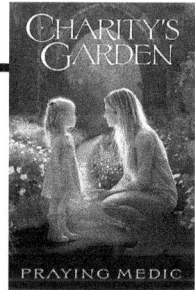

And more...

- Emotional Healing in 3 Easy Steps
- God Speaks: Perspectives on Hearing God's Voice

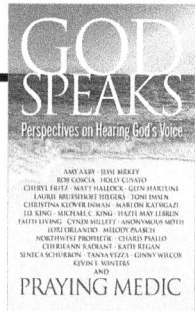